THE WANDER WOMAN'S

PHRASEBOOK

Alison Owings

Illustrated by Mary Wagstaff

Rockridge Books

an imprint of

SHAMELESS HUSSY PRESS

ISBN: 0-915288-53-2

Illustrations by Mary Wagstaff

ROCKRIDGE BOOKS

an imprint of

SHAMELESS HUSSY PRESS

Box 5540

Berkeley, California 94705

For the five star traveling companions who were there from mountain pass in Kashmir to seacoast in Spain, among other less concise highs and lows:

Annegret Hilsinger-Reinhardt, Kay McNamara Raftery, Hedi Göpfert, Ellen Hoffman, and Jonathan Perdue.

THE WANDER WOMAN'S PHRASEBOOK is supposed to amuse (well, yes, and inform) you to the point that you're not nervous about traveling to places where people have the effrontery to speak their own language.

It's meant to help provide you with the best traveling companion possible: peace of mind.

It's meant for women traveling alone, together, with a man, or with any configuration of a group.

Let us say you are walking down the street. Let us say further, an unpleasant man should begin disporting himself in an unpleasant manner.

Now, it is often difficult enough for a woman to pursue an unharassed stroll in her own country, much less where foreign tongues (or, worse, appendages) give assault. In foreign lands, one does not want to risk world peace initiatives by pummeling the creep into oblivion, nor does one want to be a stupid ninny. A rational middle ground is to say a few things back.

The ability to speak even a modicum of a foreign language is handy for more than giving hissers their comeuppance. There is, for example, the matter of the rest of the day.

And it makes an enormous difference if that day is spent in English and/or mute, or if it's spent at least partly within the language of the country you spent the time and money to see.

I once neglected to take my own advice; I considered myself well-traveled, and developed a false security about travel and foreign languages. I figured I could get around almost anywhere with what I already knew.

Then I went to Turkey.

Unable to find a Turkish phrasebook, I reassured myself that I'd be fine. On the plane, I met someone who had a phrasebook; she let me borrow it. I turned a few pages and panicked.

Not one word resembled any other word or language I knew. Good day was *iyi gunler.* Yes was *evet*; no was *hayir.* The arrogance of the west had strangled me.

Once in Istanbul, I stuck to places where I was sure someone spoke English. It was not the way I liked to wander, but Istanbul did not strike me as a place for a lone American woman to be foolhardy.

My one independent venture was to a female world: an ancient, valuted, grey marble bathhouse, where at least three generations of Turkish women could be seen in clusters through the steam, pouring water from long pitchers and having a fine old time.

That experience helped me hone a formula: the less I know a language, the less comfortable I feel in a strange culture. Even if I rarely talk, it's important that in a pinch, I'm able to.

Of course, if I were fluent in the language of every country I've visited, I'd have fewer stories. I would not have expected to see a ballet when I bought tickets in Florence to a ballata, and sat though hours of dialogue, straining to see a tutu, only to learn later that ballata is ballad. (Ballet is *balleto.*) Nor would I have asked what time the tables began in the cathedral in Seville. (Mass is *missas*; the word for tables is *mesas.*)

THE WANDER WOMAN'S PHRASEBOOK does try to keep the amusement factor in ascendance while providing you with a wealth of repartee, as well as some ho-hum phrases for ordinary needs such as finding the post office.

But its specialty is to help you ask questions of universal importance, such as, "What is your rising sign?" or, "Are you interested in poetry?"

To be able to communicate and to laugh: that's peace of mind.

Alison Owings

FRENCH

BASIC CHAT:

YES	Oui
NO	Non
PLEASE	S'il vous plaît
THANKS	Merci
HELLO	Ça va?

Hints on pronunciation:

The same vowels appear in both French and English, with the use of accents occasionally over a, e, and i.

a	ah as *lah de dah*
e	a as in *say*
i	ee as in *teeth*
o	oh as in *soap*
ou	oo as in *tool*
ue	whee as in *whee*

The consonants look like those in english, but if you try to pronounce them that way, you will get confused stares. Hors d'oeuvres is the classic example. When in doubt, swallow it, as in s'il vous plaît, which is said rather like see voo play.

ç	s as in *say*
ca, co, cu	cah as in *caught*
ge, gi	ghuh as in *rouge*
ga, go, gu	gah as in *gone*
h	silent
j	s as in *pleasure*
r	rolled
th	t as in *tea*
x	as in *excellent*, except:
x	s, in numbers six, dix, etc. which sound like cees, deese, etc.

ON THE STREET

GOOD DAY.
>Bonjour.

GOOD AFTERNOON.
>Bonjour.

GOOD EVENING.
>Bonsoir.

SAME TO YOU.
>Vous aussi.

I'M NOT INTERESTED.
>Ça ne m'intéresse pas.

IN THAT EITHER.
>Cela non plus.

STOP FOLLOWING ME.
>Arrêtez de me suivre.

YOU ARE AN INSULT TO YOUR COUNTRY.
>Vous faites honte à votre <u>pays.</u>

CITY	viille
VILLAGE	village
MOTHER.	mère.

GET AWAY.
>Fichez le camp!

LEAVE ME ALONE, YOU ANIMAL.
>Fichez-moi la paix, espèce <u>de mufle.</u>

| PIG | de cochon |
| IMBECILE | d'imbécile. |

PLEASE.

    S'il vous plaît.

IF YOU DON'T STOP

        Si vous <u>n'arrêtez pas</u>

    MOVE   ne bougez pas

    BEHAVE LIKE A GENTLEMAN,   n'agissez pas en

                                        homme bien élevé,

I'LL CALL THE POLICE.

    J'appellerai la police.

HELP!

    Au secours!

POLICE!

    Police!

I HOPE I DIDN'T HURT YOU TOO BADLY.

    J'espère ne vous avoir pas fait trop de mal.

EXCUSE ME.

    Pardon.

The underlined phrase is the section that would be replaced by the alternative phrase.

AROUND TOWN

WHERE AM I?
> Où suis-je?

WHERE IS THE BUS STATION?
> Où est <u>la station d'autobus?</u>

SUBWAY	le métro?
TRAIN STATION	la gare?
AIRPORT	l'aéroport?

MAY I GET OUT HERE?
> Puis-je descendre ici?

HOW DO I GET TO _____?
> Comment fait-on pour aller à _____?

WHERE MAY I RENT A CAR?
> Où puis-je louer une voiture?

WHERE IS A GAS STATION?
> Il y a une station service près d'ici?

FILL IT UP, PLEASE
> Le plein, s'il vous plaît.

WITH SUPER	avec super
WITH REGULAR	avec du normal
WITH DIESEL	avec du diesel

PLEASE GIVE ME _____WORTH OF REGULAR.
> Mettez _____francs d'essence normale, s'il vous plaît.

WHERE IS A PUBLIC BATH ?
> Où se trouvent les bains publics?

WHERE IS A TOILET?

    Où sont les toilettes?

WHERE IS THE MARKET?

    Où se trouve le marché?

WHEN IS IT OPEN?

    A quelle heure ouvre-t-il?

WHERE IS A BOOKSTORE?

    Y a t'il <u>une librairie près d'ici?</u>

TRAVEL BUREAU

    une agence de voyages près d'ici?

BANK

    une banque près d'ici?

POST OFFICE

    un bureau de poste près d'ici?

AIRMAIL STAMPS, PLEASE.

    Il me faut des timbres pour le courrier aérien.

WHERE MAY I MAKE A LOCAL TELEPHONE CALL?

    Où puis-je <u>téléphoner en ville</u>

LONG DISTANCE   téléphoner à l'étranger?

DO YOU KNOW WHERE THE AMERICAN EMBASSY IS?

    Pouvez-vous me dire où se trouve <u>l'Ambassade</u>

    <u>américaine?</u>

CONSULATE   le Consulat américain

AMERICAN EXPRESS OFFICE   le bureau de

    l'american express

A HOSPITAL   un hôpital?

A DRUGSTORE   une pharmacie près

    d'ici?

I NEED A DOCTOR ... WHO SPEAKS ENGLISH.

Je cherche un docteur ...qui parle anglais.

DO YOU SELL ANYTHING FOR HEADACHES?

Vous avez quelque chose pour les maux de tête?

DIARRHEA	contre la diarrhée
CONSTIPATION	contre la constipation
SUNBURN	pour les coups de soleil?

DO YOU SELL SOAP?

Vous vendez du savon?

SHAMPOO	du shampoing?
DEODORANT	des désodorisants
DIAPHRAGM CREAM	des crèmes pour diaphragmes
CONDOMS	des préservatifs
TAMPONS	des tampons périodiques
SANITARY NAPKINS	des serviettes higiéniques
TOOTHPASTE	du dentifrice
TOOTHBRUSHES	des brosses à dents
TALCUM POWDER	du talc
SUNTAN LOTION	des produits solaires?

WHERE MIGHT I FIND A GYM?

Y a t'il une salle de gymnastique près d'ici?

BEAUTY PARLOR	un salon de beauté
MOVIE THEATER	un cinéma
THEATER	un théâtre près d'ici
MUSIC	un endroit où on joue de la musique
A PLACE TO DANCE	une discotheque
POOL HALL	un billard

VIDEO GAMES ARCADE une salle de jeux
électroniques

WHERE MIGHT I FIND A MASSEUSE?
Pourriez-vous me donner l'addresse d'une masseuse?

WHERE IS A FORTUNE TELLER?
Où pourrais-je trouver une voyante?

DO YOU KNOW OF A GOOD, CHEAP, UNDERRATED RESTAURANT
Connaissez-vous un bon petit resto pas trop cher?
RESTAURANT UNKNOWN TO TOURISTS?
un restaurant peu frequenté par les touristes?

WHERE IS THE ACTION AT NIGHT?
Où peut -on se divertir le soir?

IS IT SAFE FOR A WOMAN BY HERSELF?
Est-ce qu'une femme peut sortir toute seule sans crainte?
FOR WOMEN que les femmes peuvent sortir toutes
seules sans crainte?
FOR AMERICANS que les américains peuvent sortir tous
seuls sans crainte?
IS IT EXPENSIVE?
Est-ce que c'est cher?

HOW DO I GET THERE?
Comment y va-t'on?

WOULD YOU WRITE IT DOWN, PLEASE?
Pouvez-vous écrire ça sur un morceau de papier?

DOES ANYONE SPEAK ENGLISH?
Y a t'il quelqu'un qui parle anglais?

BUYING, OR NOT

MAY I HELP YOU?
>Je peux vous aider?

I HAVE NOT DECIDED.
>Je n'ai pas décidé.

I'M JUST BROWSING FOR NOW.
>Je veux simplement regarder pour le moment.

IS THAT ALL RIGHT?
>Ça ne vous dérange pas?

I WILL HELP YOU.
>Je vais vous aider.

I WON'T BUY ANYTHING, IF YOU PESTER ME.
>Je n'achèterai rien si vous me dérangez.

DID YOU MAKE IT?
>C'est vous qui l'avez <u>fait?</u>
>GROW IT?   produit?

HOW MUCH DOES THIS COST?
>Ce coûte combien?

HOW MUCH FOR TWO OF THEM?
>Combien <u>pour les deux?</u>
>ALL OF THEM?   pour le tout?

MAY I TASTE IT?
>Je peux en goûter un petit morceau?

MAY I TRY IT ON?

    Je peux l'essayer?

TOO BIG.

    C'est trop grand.

TOO SMALL.

    C'est trop petit.

IT SUITS YOU EXACTLY.

    Ça vous va à merveille.

I BET.

    Vous plàisantez!

VERY NICE.

    C'est très joli.

I'LL TAKE IT.

    Je la prends.

I'LL TAKE A KILO.

    Je vais en prendre un kilo.

DO YOU ACCEPT TRAVELLERS' CHECKS?

    Vous prenez les "travelers checks?"

    CREDIT CARDS?   les cartes de crédit?

    U.S. DOLLARS?   les dollars?

AM I EXPECTED TO BARGAIN?

    Peut-on marchander?

IT'S TOO EXPENSIVE FOR ME.

    C'est trop cher pour moi.

I HAVE LITTLE MONEY.

    Je n'ai pas beaucoup d'argent.

I'M NEARLY BROKE.

    Je suis presque fauché.

THE TRUTH IS, I DON'T LIKE IT.

    A vrai dire, <u>ça ne me plaît pas.</u>

| DON'T NEED IT | je n'en ai pas besoin. |
| DON'T WANT IT | je n'en ai pas envie. |

PERHAPS I'LL COME BACK ANOTHER TIME.

    Je repasserai peut-être une autre fois.

EATING OUT

I WOULD LIKE A TABLE FOR ONE

Vous avez une table <u>pour une personne?</u>

TWO	pour deux
THREE	pour trois
FOUR, PLEASE.	pour quatre, s'il vous plaît.

I WOULD LIKE TODAY'S SPECIALTY, PLEASE.

Je voudrais <u>le plat du jour, s'il vous plaît.</u>

TODAY'S SOUP	la soupe du jour
SOME BREAD	du pain
A VEGETARIAN MEAL	un repas végétarien
SOME WATER	un verre d'eau
FRUIT JUICE	un jus de fruit
A BEER	une bière
SOME EGGS	des oeufs

I WOULD LIKE SOMETHING LIGHT.

J'aimerais <u>quelque chose de léger.</u>

SOMETHING FILLING	Quelque chose de substantiel
SOMETHING SPECIAL TO THIS AREA	une specialité du pays
SOME CHEESE	un peu de fromage
A GLASS OF LOCAL WINE	un verre de vin du pays
A BOTTLE OF LOCAL WINE	un bouteille de vin du pays
DESSERT	prendre un dessert.
A CUP OF COFFEE , PLEASE	un café, s'il vous plaît.
A CUP OF TEA	un thé, s'il vous plaît

I WANT TO BUY THAT MAN A DRINK.

Je voudrais offrir un verre à <u>ce monsieur-là.</u>

I WANT TO BUY THAT WOMAN A DRINK.
Je voudrais offrir un verre à cette dame-là.

MAY I GET YOU SOMETHING TO EAT?
Puis-je vous offrir quelque chose à manger?

I AM NOT THIRSTY, THANKS.
Je n'ai pas soif, merci.

I AM NOT HUNGRY, THANKS.
Je n'ai pas faim, merci.

WAITER
Monsieur

WAITRESS
Mademoiselle

THE CHECK, PLEASE.
L'addition, s'il vous plait.

LET ME PAY.
Laissez-moi payer.

LET ME PAY FOR MY SHARE.
Laissez-moi payer ma consommation.

ONLY IF YOU INSIST.
Seulement si vous insistez.

I INSIST.
Oui, j'insiste.

ARE YOU INSISTENT ABOUT EVERYTHING?
>   Est-ce que vous insistez à propos de tout?

TRY ME.
>   Essayez voir.

DON'T TRY ME.
>   Ne me tentez pas.

MY COMPLIMENTS TO THE CHEF.
>   Mes compliments au chef.

I AM NOT FEELING WELL.
>   Je ne me sens pas très bien.

WHERE IS THE REST ROOM?
>   Où sont les toilettes?

MEN
>   Messieurs

WOMEN
>   Dames

ROCK BOTTOM BUDGET

MAY I CAMP HERE?

      Est-ce que je peux camper <u>ici</u>?

    THERE?   là-bas?

MAY WE CAMP HERE?

    Pouvons-nous camper ici?

        MAY WE CAMP THERE?

           Pouvons-nous camper là-bas?

I HAVE A SLEEPING BAG.

      <u>J'ai un sac</u> de couchage.

   WE HAVE   Nous avons des sacs de couchage.

I HAVE A TENT.

   J'ai une tente.

ARE FIRES PERMISSABLE?

   Peut - on faire un feu de camp ici?

IS THE WATER SAFE TO DRINK?

   Est-ce que l'eau est potable?

MAY I SING IN EXCHANGE FOR A MEAL?

   Puis-je payer pour le repas?

WOULD YOU ACCEPT THIS IN EXCHANGE FOR A MEAL?

    Pourriez-vous accepter ceci pour le prix <u>du repas?</u>

   FOR A ROOM?   de la chambre?

I AM NOT FOR BARTER.   WE ARE NOT FOR BARTER.

   Je ne suis pas à vendre.   Nous ne sommes pas à vendre.

HOW DARE YOU.

    Pour qui me prenez vous?

THANKS ANYWAY.

    Merci quand même.

" MAY WE CAMP THERE? "

MISCELLANEOUS ESSENTIALS AND NON-ESSENTIALS

MONEY: Franc

0.	zéro
1.	un
2.	deux
3.	trois
4.	quatre
5.	cinq
6.	six
7.	sept
8.	huit
9.	neuf
10.	dix
11.	onze
12.	douze
13.	treize
14.	quatorze
15.	quinze
16.	seize
17.	dix-sept
18.	dix-huit
19.	dix-neuf
20.	vingt
21.	vingt-et-un
22.	vingt-deux
30.	trente
40.	quarante
50.	cinquante
60.	soixante
70.	soixante-dix
80.	quatre-vingts
90.	quatre-vingt-dix

100.	cent
200.	deux cents
1000.	mille
1100	onze cents
2000	deux mille
10,000	dix mille
100,000	cent mille
1,000,000	un million

WHAT TIME IS IT?
  Quelle heure est-il?

NOON.
  Midi.

MIDNIGHT.
  Minuit.

ONE O'CLOCK IN THE AFTERNOON.
  Une heure de l'après-midi.

ONE O'CLOCK IN THE MORNING.
  Une heure du matin.

TWO O'CLOCK   TEN TO TWO.
  Deux heures   deux heures moins dix.

TEN PAST TWO   QUARTER PAST TWO.
  Deux heures dix   deux heures et quart.

HALF PAST TWO   QUARTER OF TWO.
  Deux heures et demie   deux heures moins le quart.

MAY I SEE YOUR WATCH, PLEASE?
  Puis-je voir votre montre, s'il vous plaît?

DAYS, SEASONS & MONTHS

SUNDAY	Dimanche
MONDAY	Lundi
TUESDAY	Mardi
WEDNESDAY	Mercredi
THURSDAY	Jeudi
FRIDAY	Vendredi
SATURDAY	Samedi

SPRING	le printemps
SUMMER	l'été
FALL	l'automne
WINTER	l'hiver

JANUARY	Janvier
FEBRUARY	Fevrier
MARCH	Mars
APRIL	Avril
MAY	Mai
JUNE	Juin
JULY	Juillet
AUGUST	Août
SEPTEMBER	Septembre
OCTOBER	Octobre
NOVEMBER	Novembre
DECEMBER	Décembre

COLORS

	Masculine	Feminine
RED	rouge	
ORANGE	orange	
YELLOW	jaune	
GREEN	vert	verte
BLUE	bleu	bleue
PURPLE	violet	violette
PINK	rose	
BROWN	marron	
BEIGE	beige	
GREY	gris	grise
BLACK	noir	noire
WHITE	blanc	blanche

COME ONS AND TURN OFFS

HAVEN'T WE MET BEFORE?
> Ne s'est-on pas déja rencontrés?

WHAT'S A MAN LIKE YOU DOING IN A PLACE LIKE THIS?
> Que fait un type comme vous dans un tel endroit?

ARE YOU WAITING FOR SOMEONE?
> Vous attendez quelqu'un?

IS THIS YOUR FIRST TRIP TO _____?
> C'est votre premier voyage en _____?

ARE YOU ENJOYING IT?
> Ça vous plaît?

HAVE YOU VISITED_____?
> Avez vous visité_____?

WHAT A PITY!
> Quel dommage!

DO YOU LIKE THE FRENCH PEOPLE?
> Est-ce que vous trouvez les français sympathiques?

THE AMERICAN PEOPLE   les americaines

MAY I SIT WITH YOU?
> Je peux m'asseoir à côté de vous?

MAY I BE YOUR GUIDE?
> Puis-je vous servir de guide?

MAY I TAKE YOU DANCING?
> Puis-je vous inviter à aller danser?

WOULD YOU LIKE TO WALK IN THE MOONLIGHT?
Voulez-vous faire une promenade au clair de lune?

WOULD YOU LIKE TO SEE WHERE I LIVE?
Voulez-vous voir où j'habite?

YOU AMERICAN WOMEN ARE SO FORWARD.
Vous, les Américaines, vous êtes si sans gêne!

YES.
Oui.

NO.
Non.

HARDLY.
Pas du tout.

I'D LIKE THAT.
Oui, je veux bien.

I DO NOT SPEAK FRENCH.
Je ne parle pas français.

I WISH TO BE ALONE.
Je voudrais être seule.

I AM TRYING TO THINK.
Je suis en train de réfléchir.
TO READ.   de lire.

I AM TRYING TO SLEEP.
Je veux dormir.

I PREFER MY OWN COMPANY, IF YOU DON'T MIND.

Je préfère être seule, si ça vous fait rien.

PLEASE DO NOT DISTURB ME.

Ne me dérangez pas!

I HAVE AN EXTREMELY CONTAGIOUS DISEASE.

Je souffre d'une maladie extrêmement contagieuse.

WHAT IS YOUR NAME?

Quel est votre nom?

MY NAME IS _____.

Je m'appelle_____.

HOW VERY AMERICAN.

Ça c'est typiquement américain.

FRENCH	français
GERMAN	allemand
ITALIAN	italien
SPANISH	espagnol.

WHERE ARE YOU FROM?

D'où êtes-vous?

I AM FROM THE UNITED STATES.

Je viens des Etats-Unis.

EAST OF THE SUN AND WEST OF THE MOON

de l'est du soleil et de l'ouest de la lune.

A SMALL TOWN.   d'une petite ville.

WHAT INTERESTS YOU IN LIFE?

Qu'est ce que vous intéresse dans la vie?

WHAT ARE YOU SEEKING?

    Vous êtes à la recherche de quoi?

AN ECSTATIC MOMENT	d'un moment d'extase
ART	d'art
ASTROLOGY	d'astrologie
BUSINESS	d'affaires
COOKING	de cuisine
CONTRADICTIONS	de contrastes
DANCING	de danse
DREAMS	de rêves
ECOLOGY	d'écologie
EXCITEMENT	d'aventure
EXERCISE	d'exercice
FEMINISM	de féminisme
FILM	de cinéma
HAPPINESS	de bonheur

I WOULD LIKE TO GET HOME SAFELY.

    Je veux rentrer chez moi sans risque d'être agressée.

INCONSEQUENTIAL MATTERS, TO YOU, PROBABLY.

    De choses sans importance, pour vous, probablement.

LIBERAL CAUSES	de causes libérales

LIFE, LOVE, AND THE PURSUIT OF HAPPINESS.

    de vie, d'amour, et de bonheur

MONEY	d'argent
MUSIC	de musique
NOTHING MUCH	de rien de special
POETRY	de poésie
POLITICS	de politique
POWER	de pouvoir
QUIET	de tranquillité

READING	de lecture
RELIGION	de religion
SAVING THE WORLD.	du moyen de sauver le monde.
SEX	de sexe
SPORTS	de sports
THE PERFECT WAVE	de la vague parfaite
THE THEATER	de théâtre
THEATRICS	de drame
TRUTH	de vérité
VAGARIES OF THE UNIVERSE	des caprices de l'univers
YOU	vous *formal*
	tu *familiar*

FASCINATING!

Passionnant!

I DO NOT BELIEVE IT.

Je ne le crois pas.

WHAT ASTROLOGICAL SIGN ARE YOU?

Quel est votre signe du zodiac?

WHAT IS YOUR RISING SIGN?

Quel est votre signe ascendant?

AQUARIUS	verseau
PISCES	poissons
ARIES	bélier
TAURUS	taureau

GEMINI	gémeaux
CANCER	cancer
LEO	lion
VIRGO	vierge

LIBRA	balance
SCORPIO	scorpion
SAGITARRIUS	sagittaire
CAPRICORN	capricorne

I DON'T KNOW WHAT YOU'RE TALKING ABOUT.

Je ne comprends pas ce que vous dites.

WHAT KIND OF WOMAN DO YOU ENJOY?

Quel type de femme aimez-vous?

I AM MORE INTERESTED IN INTELLIGENCE
        Ce qui m'attire c'est <u>l'intelligence</u>

CHARM	le charme
HUMOR	le sens de l'humour
SEX	le sexe

...THAN I AM IN CHARM
        m'attire plus que <u>le charme.</u>

INTELLIGENCE	l'intelligence
HUMOR	le sens de l'humour
SEX.	le sexe.

ARE YOU TRYING TO GET OVER A ROMANCE?
    Est-ce que vous essayez d'oublier une liaison rompue?

I AM TRYING TO GET OVER A ROMANCE.
    J'essaie d'oublier une liaison rompue.

HOW ROMANTIC.
    Que c'est romantique.

I AM NOT ROMANTIC.
    Moi, je ne suis pas romantique.

ARE YOU MARRIED?
    Etes-vous marié?

I AM MARRIED.
    Je suis mariée.

I AM NOT MARRIED.
    Je ne suis pas mariée.

SORT OF.
    En quelque sorte, je le suis.

FORTUNATELY, NO.
Heureusement pas.

UNFORTUNATELY, NO.
Malheureusement pas.

I AM SINGLE.
Je suis célibataire.

I AM SINGLE, BUT LIVING WITH SOMEONE
Je suis célibataire mais je vis avec quelqu'un.

I AM SEPARATED.
Je suis séparée.
DIVORCED   divorcée
WIDOWED.   veuve.

DO YOU HAVE ANY CHILDREN?
Vous avez des enfants?

FORTUNATELY, NO.
Heureusement non.

UNFORTUNATELY, NO.
Malheureusement non.

I HAVE ONE CHILD.   TWO
J'ai un enfant.   J'ai deux enfants.

            THREE   MANY CHILDREN.
            trois enfants.   beaucoup d'enfants.

ARE YOU HOMOSEXUAL?
Etes vous homosexuelle? *fem.*   homosexuel? *masc.*

30

I AM HOMOSEXUAL.
 Je suis homosexuelle.

I AM NOT HOMOSEXUAL.
 Je ne suis pas homosexuelle.

I MIGHT BECOME HOMOSEXUAL SOON.
 Il se peut que je devienne bientôt homosexuelle.

IT IS NONE OF YOUR BUSINESS.
 Ça ne vous regarde pas!

GUESS.
 Devinez.

DO YOU CONSIDER YOURSELF A FEMINIST?
 Vous considérez vous comme une féministe?
 A SEXIST? une sexiste?

WOULD YOU LIKE TO DISCUSS IT?
 Est-ce que vous aimeriez en discuter?

IS THERE A FEMINIST ORGANIZATION HERE?
 Y a-t'il une organisation féministe ici?

IS IT POSSIBLE TO MEET SOME FEMINIST WOMEN
 Est-il possible de rencontrer des femmes féministes?
 ...SOME FEMINIST MEN?
 d'hommes féministes?

DO YOU THINK THAT MEN AND WOMEN SHOULD BE EDUCATED THE
SAME?
 Croyez-vous que les hommes et les femmes
 devraient avoir la même éducation?

PAID THE SAME?

    devraient avoir le même salaire?

TREATED THE SAME?

    devraient être traités de la même façon?

WHY NOT?

    Pourquoi pas?

OF COURSE!

    Mais naturellement!

THAT IS CONTRARY TO THE LAWS OF NATURE.

    Cela va à l'encontre des lois de la nature.

YOU LOOK BEAUTIFUL.

    Vous êtes beau *to a man*   belle *to a woman*

...WHEN YOU'RE ANGRY.

    quand vous êtes en colère.

IT SEEMS WE HAVE LITTLE IN COMMON.

    Nous n'avons pas l'air d'avoir grand' chose en commun.

IT SEEMS WE HAVE MUCH IN COMMON.

    Je crois que nous avons beaucoup de points communs.

IN YOUR COUNTRY, ARE MOST MEN LIKE YOU?

    Est-ce que la plupart des hommes sont comme vous dans
        votre pays?

IN MY COUNTRY, MOST WOMEN ARE LIKE ME.

    Dans mon pays la plupart des femmes sont comme moi.

SHALL WE SEE EACH OTHER AGAIN?

    Peut-on se revoir?

WHAT A RIDICULOUS IDEA!

               Quelle idée bizarre!

    HOPELESS   ridicule

    HORRIBLE   horrible

    INSPIRED!   géniale!

WHERE SHALL WE MEET?

    Où peut-on se retrouver?

AT MY PLACE

    Chez moi.

           YOUR PLACE.

                 Chez toi.

IN PUBLIC.

    Dans un endroit public.

HOW ABOUT A LARGE CAFE?

           Si on se rencontrait dans un grand café?

SOMEWHERE WHERE WE CAN BE ALONE

         un coin où on peut être seuls

A DIVE   une boîte mal famée

SOMEWHERE REDOLENT OF UNRESTRAINED PASSION & INTRIGUE

         un lieu plein de passion déchaînée et d'intrigue

A PLACE WITH LIVE MUSIC un endroit où on joue de la musique

A RESTAURANT FAVORED BY WEAK-STOMACHED TOURISTS

    un restaurant recherché par les touristes à l'estomac délicat

A PLACE WHERE YOU'D TAKE YOUR PARENTS

        un endroit où vous aimeriez amener vos parents

ANYWHERE WITH A VIEW   un endroit où il y a une jolie vue

HOW ABOUT SURPRISING ME?

    Faites-moi la surprise.

LET ME SURPRISE YOU.

    Laissez-moi vous faire la surprise.

I BEG YOUR PARDON.

    Je vous demande pardon.

WHEN SHALL WE MEET?

    Quand peut-on se voir?

THE EARLIER THE BETTER.

    Le plus tôt possible.

        THE LATER THE BETTER.

            Le plus tard possible.

SHALL I BRING A CHAPERONE?

    Dois-je venir avec un chaperon?

YOU ARE TOO FUNNY.

    Que vous êtes drôle.

I'VE ALWAYS DEPENDED UPON THE KINDNESS OF STRANGERS.

    J'ai toujours eu recours à la gentillesse des gens.

IS THAT FROM A PLAY?

    Avez-vous sorti ça d'une pièce de théâtre?

THAT IS FROM A PLAY.

        Ça c'est tiré d'une pièce de théâtre.

YOU ARE TOO CLEVER.

    Vous êtes trop malin.

GOODBYE FOR NOW.

    A bientôt.

SLEEPING ARRANGEMENTS

IS THERE A CHEAP HOTEL NEARBY?

Y a-t'il <u>un hôtel pas trop cher près d'ici?</u>

CLEAN   un hôtel propre près d'ici

GOOD   un bon hôtel près d'ici?

WHERE IS THE NEAREST YOUTH HOSTEL?

Où se trouve l'auberge de jeunesse la plus proche?

DO YOU KNOW WHERE I COULD RENT A ROOM?

Pourriez-vous me dire où je peux louer une chambre?

FOR HOW MANY DAYS?

Pour combien de jours?

JUST FOR TONIGHT   pour ce soir seulement

FOR A WEEK   pour une semaine

FOR A MONTH   pour un mois.

HOW MUCH DOES THE ROOM COST?

Combien coûte la chambre?

DOES IT HAVE A NICE VIEW?

Est-ce qu'elle a une jolie vue?

IS IT QUIET?

Est-ce que c'est calme

I'D LIKE SOMETHING THAT EVOKES THE ROMANCE OF AGES PAST.

J'aimerais quelque chose qui évoque le charme des temps passés.

I HAVE JUST THE ROOM FOR YOU.

J'ai la chambre qu'il vous faut.

I'M SORRY; WE HAVE MODERNIZED.

Je regrette, nous avons tout modernisé.

I WANT A PRIVATE BATH.

Je voudrais une chambre avec un bain ou douche.

I DO NOT WANT A PRIVATE BATH.

Je n'ai pas besoin d'une salle de bain privée.

WE WOULD LIKE A DOUBLE BED.

Nous voudrions un lit pour deux personnes.

TWIN BEDS.   deux lits separés.

IS BREAKFAST INCLUDED?

Est-ce que le petit déjeuner est compris?

MAY I SEE THE ROOM PLEASE?   HAVE YOU ANY OTHERS?

Puis-je voir la chambre?   Avez-vous d'autres chambres?

THANK YOU FOR YOUR TROUBLE

Merci, et excusez-moi de vous avoir dérangé.

FINE, I'LL TAKE IT.

Très bien, je vais la prendre.

FINE, WE'LL TAKE IT.

Très bien, nous allons la prendre

WHEN IS CHECK OUT TIME?

A quelle heure faut-il quitter la chambre?

I WOULD LIKE SOME SOAP, PLEASE.

Je voudrais une savonette, s'il vous plaît.

SOME TOWELS   des serviettes de bain

SOME DRINKING WATER   une carafe d'eau

A BLANKET   une couverture.

I WOULD LIKE SOME QUIET.

J'ai besoin de tranquillité et de silence.

THE KEY TO ROOM _____, PLEASE.

La clé de la chambre _____, s'il vous plaît.

ARE THERE ANY MESSAGES FOR ME?

Y a-t'il des messages pour moi?

I AM EXPECTING A VISITOR.

J'attends un visiteur.

COME IN.

Entrez.

" THE KEY TO ROOM 3, PLEASE. "

INTIMACIES

HOW GOOD TO SEE YOU.
Quel plaisir de te revoir!

MY DEAR.

to a friend   mon cher *to a man*   ma chère *to a woman*
to a lover   mon chéri   ma chérie.

HOW ARE YOU?
Comment vas-tu?

I AM WONDERFUL

Je suis <u>superbien.</u>

TERRIBLE	très mal
AS YOU SEE	comme tu me vois
NERVOUS	tendue
EAGER	pleine d'entrain
TIRED	fatiguée
TIRED BUT NOT TOO TIRED	fatiguée mais pas trop.

I AM BUT PUTTY IN YOUR HANDS
Je suis comme de la cire molle dans tes bras.

I AM A SHADOW OF MY FORMER SELF.
Je suis l'ombre de moi-même.

LET ME BE THE JUDGE OF THAT.
Laissez-moi juger par moi-même.

YOU FOOL.
Espèce <u>d'idiot!</u> *to a man*   d'idiote! *to a woman.*

DO YOU MIND IF I LOCK THE DOOR?
Ça te dérange <u>si je ferme la porte à clé?</u>

DO YOU MIND IF I PULL THE CURTAINS CLOSED?

Ça te dérange <u>si je tire les rideaux?</u>

IF I PULL THE CURTAINS OPEN	si j'ouvre les rideaux
SEND THE SERVANTS AWAY	si je renvoie les domestiques
MAKE MYSELF COMFORTABLE	si je mets à l'aise
DOUSE THE INCENSE	si j'éteins l'encens
TURN DOWN THE VOLUME	si je baisse le son
TURN UP THE VOLUME	j'augmente le son

DO YOU MIND IF I RECONSIDER?

Ça t'ennuie si <u>je reviens sur ma décision?</u>

INTRODUCE YOU TO A FRIEND je te présente <u>à une amie?</u>

if the friend is a woman

à un ami?

if the friend is a man

SHALL WE UNDRESS?

On se déshabille?

SHALL WE NOT UNDRESS?

On reste habillés?

LET'S NOT HURRY.

Ne nous pressons pas.

LET'S NOT WASTE TIME.

Ne perdons pas de temps.

ARE YOU CLEAN?

Tu n'a pas de maladies, j'espère?

ARE YOU SURE?

Tu es sûr et certain?

DO YOU KNOW WHAT I MEAN?
>   Tu sais ce que j'entends par ça?

I CONSIDER THAT AN INSULT.
>   Je prends ça pour une insulte.

I'M SURE YOU DO.
>   J'en suis sûre.

I LOVE YOUR EYES.	J'adore <u>tes yeux.</u>
HAIR	tes cheveux
MOUTH	ta bouche
TONGUE	ta langue
FACE	ton visage
RIGHT SHOULDER	ton épaule droite
SKIN	ta peau
FEET	tes pieds
IMPERFECTIONS	tes imperfections
STOMACH	ton ventre
SMELL	ton odeur
UNDERWEAR	tes dessous
ENERGY	ton énergie
PERSISTANCE.	ta persistance.

I LOVE YOU.
>   Je t'aime.

I LOVE YOU, BUT I DON'T LIKE YOU.
>   Je t'aime, mais je ne te trouve pas très sympa.

I LIKE YOU, BUT I DON'T LOVE YOU.
>   Je te trouve sympa, mais je ne t'aime pas d'amour.

YOUR KISSES ARE DIVINE.
Tes baisers sont divins.

YOUR KISSES ARE UNUSUAL.
Tes baisers sont originaux.

THIS IS MY FIRST TIME.
C'est la première fois pour moi.

IS THIS YOUR FIRST TIME?
C'est la première fois pour toi?

I CONSIDER THAT AN INSULT.
Tu m'insultes!

HAVE YOU CHANGED YOUR MIND?
Est-ce que tu as changé d'avis?

NOT EXACTLY.
Pas tout à fait.

I HAVE CHANGED MY MIND.
J'ai changé d'avis.

PERHAPS WE CAN BE FRIENDS.
Peut-être pouvons-nous juste être amis.

I MUST MAKE CERTAIN I WILL NOT GET PREGNANT.
Je dois m'assurer de ne pas tomber enceinte.

I DIDN'T MEAN THAT.
Ce n'est pas ce que je voulais dire.

AM I HURTING YOU?
Est-ce que je te fais mal?

41

YES.
> Oui.

NO.
> Non.

A LITTLE.
> Un peu.

SURELY YOU JEST.
> Tu plaisantes, non?

WE ARE LIKE TWO SHIPS PASSING IN THE NIGHT.
> Nous sommes comme <u>deux navires qui se rencontrent dans la nuit.</u>
>
> A PAIR OF LOVE BIRDS deux oiseaux amoureux
> A SYMPHONY OF THE SENSES une symphonie des sens
> A BAD MOVIE un mauvais film.

HOW ORIGINAL!
> Que c'est original!

WHY ARE YOU READING FROM THE LITTLE BOOK?
> Pourquoi est-ce que tu consultes le petit livre?

DO YOU LIKE THIS?
> Tu aimes ça?

WHAT?
> Quoi?

I DO NOT LIKE THAT.
> Je n'aime pas ça.

I LIKE THAT.
J'aime ça.

ONE MORE TIME.
Encore une fois.

LET ME DO THAT.
Laisse-moi faire ça.

WHAT ABOUT ME?
Et moi, alors?

I FORGOT.
J'ai oublié.

PATIENCE IS A VIRTUE.
La patience est une vertu.

HOW EXQUISITE!
Comme c'est exquis!

IT DOESN'T MATTER.
Ça n'a pas d'importance.

THAT TICKLES.
Oh, ça chatouille!

I'M NOT LAUGHING AT YOU.
Je ne me moque pas de toi.

THERE IS NO BETTER PLACE TO LAUGH THAN IN BED.
Il n'y a pas de meilleur endroit pour rire que dans un lit.

WHAT IS SO FUNNY?
Qu'y a-t'il de si drôle?

EVERYTHING / NOTHING.
>Tout / rien.

THAT WAS MY FIRST TIME.
>C'était la première fois pour moi.

WAS THAT YOUR FIRST TIME?
>Pour toi, c'était la   première fois?

I FIND THAT DIFFICULT TO BELIEVE.
>Je trouve ça difficile à croire.

LET'S GO TO SLEEP.
>Fermons les yeux et dormons.

LET'S NOT GO TO SLEEP.
>Ne nous endormons pas.

IT'S A PITY WE DON'T SPEAK THE SAME LANGUAGE.
>Quel dommage qu'on ne parle pas la même langue!

I'M GLAD WE SPEAK THE SAME LANGUAGE.
>Je suis content qu'on parle la même langue.

ARE YOU TIRED?
>Tu es fatigué?

I AM TIRED.
>Je suis fatigué.

I NEVER TIRE.
>Moi, je ne me fatigue jamais.

GOOD MORNING.
>Bonjour.

ITALIAN

"WHERE AM I ?"

BASIC CHAT:

YES	Si
NO	No
PLEASE	Per piacere
THANKS	Grazie
HELLO	Buon giorno

Hints on pronunciation:

The same vowels appear in both Italian and English, with one (è) written with an accent.

a	ah	*as in shah*
è	eh	*as in set*
e	a	*as in say*
i	ee	*as in teeth*
o	oh	*as in soap*
u	oo	*as in tool*

The consonants are rather as they are in English, except that z is pronounced as it is in German: ts.

ca	cah	*as in caught*
ce	che	*as in ché*
che	kay	*as in okay*
chi	kee	*as in keep*
ci	chee	*as in cheat*
co	co	*as in co-op*

ge	jay	*as in jay*
gh	ghe	*as spaghetti*
gi	ghee	*as in jeez*
gli	eyon	*as in billion*

sce	sh	*as in swish*

z	ts	*as in pizza*

ON THE STREET

GOOD DAY.
> Buon giorno.

GOOD AFTERNOON.
> Buon pomeriggio.

GOOD EVENING.
> Buona sera.

SAME TO YOU.
> Lo stesso a te.

I'M NOT INTERESTED.
> Non sono interessata.

IN THAT, EITHER.
> Anche in quello.

STOP FOLLOWING ME.
> Lasciami da sola *fem.*
>> solo *masc.*

GET AWAY.
> Vai via.

YOU ARE AN INSULT TO YOUR COUNTRY.
> Sei un insulto <u>al tuo paese.</u>

CITY	alla tua città
VILLAGE	a tuo villaggio
MOTHER.	per tua madre.

LEAVE ME ALONE, YOU ANIMAL.

Lasciami da sola, <u>animale che sei.</u>

PIG   porco che sei.

IMBECILE   imbecille che sei.

PLEASE.

Per favore.

IF YOU DON'T STOP,

Se non ti <u>fermi,</u>

MOVE   muovi

BEHAVE LIKE A GENTLEMAN   comporti come un

                                             gentiluomo,

...I'LL CALL THE POLICE!

chiamerò la polizia!

HELP!

Aiuto!

POLICE!

Polizia!

I HOPE I DIDN'T HURT YOU TOO BADLY.

Spero che non ti ho fatto male.

EXCUSE ME.

Scusami.

AROUND TOWN

WHERE AM I?
> Dove sono?

WHERE IS THE BUS STATION?
>> Dov'è <u>la stazione d'autobus?</u>

SUBWAY	la metropolitana
TRAIN STATION	la stazione dei treni
AIRPORT	l'aeroporto?

MAY I GET OUT HERE?
> Posso uscire di qua?

HOW DO I GET TO ____?
> Come arrivo a____?

WHERE MAY I RENT A CAR?
> Dove posso affittare un automobile?

WHERE IS A GAS STATION?
> C'è una stazione di servizio?

FILL IT UP, PLEASE
>> Il pieno, per favore

WITH SUPER	con super
WITH REGULAR	con normale
WITH DIESEL.	con diesel.

PLEASE GIVE ME____WORTH OF REGULAR.
> Voglio____di normale.

WHERE IS A PUBLIC BATH ?
> C'è un <u>bagno publico qua vicino?</u>
> A TOILET?   servizio publico qua vicino?

WHERE IS THE MARKET?	WHEN DOES IT OPEN?
Dov'è il mercato?	Quali sono gli orari?

WHERE IS A BOOKSTORE?

Dov' è una libreria?

TRAVEL BUREAU	una agenzia di viaggio
POST OFFICE	un ufficio postale?
BANK	una banca

AIRMAIL STAMPS, PLEASE.

Francobolli per posta aerea per favore.

WHERE MAY I MAKE A LOCAL • LONG DISTANCE TELEPHONE CALL?

Dove posso fare una chiamata locale?

Dove posso fare una chiamata interurbana?

DO YOU KNOW WHERE THE AMERICAN EMBASSY IS?

Potrebbe dirmi dove si trova l'Ambasciata Americana?

CONSULATE	il Consolato Americano
AMERICAN EXPRESS OFFICE	l'ufficio dell' American Express
A HOSPITAL	un ospedale
A DOCTOR	un dottore
...ONE WHO SPEAKS ENGLISH	...che parla inglese
A DRUGSTORE	una farmacia?

DO YOU SELL ANYTHING FOR HEADACHES?

Vendete medicina per il mal di testa?

DIARRHEA	la diarrea
CONSTIPATION	la costipazione intestinale
SUNBURN	l'usti one

DO YOU SELL SOAP?

Avete <u>sapone?</u>

SHAMPOO	shampo
DEODORANT	deodorante
DIAPHRAGM CREAM	la crema spermicida
CONDOMS	preservativi
TAMPONS	tamponi
SANITARY NAPKINS	assorbenti
TOOTHPASTE	dentifricio
TOOTHBRUSHES	spazzolino da denti
TALCUM POWDER	talco
SUNTAN LOTION	olio abbronzante

WHERE MIGHT I FIND A GYM?

C'è <u>una palestra?</u>

BEAUTY PARLOR	un instituto di bellezza
FORTUNE TELLER	un' indovina
MASSEUSE	una massaggiatrice
MOVIE THEATER	un cinema
THEATER	un teatro
MUSIC	un locale dove suonano la musica
A PLACE TO DANCE	un locale dove si balla
A POOL HALL	un sala da biliardo
VIDEO GAMES ARCADE	un galleria con i video giochi

GOOD, CHEAP, UNDERRATED RESTAURANT?

un buon ristorante economico e non conosciuto?

RESTAURANT UNKNOWN TO PEOPLE LIKE ME?

un ristorante non conosciuto a gente come me?

WHERE IS THE ACTION AT NIGHT?

Dove si va di sera?

IS IT SAFE FOR A WOMAN BY HERSELF?
                    `E pericoloso per una donna da sola?
    FOR WOMEN   per donne
    FOR AMERICANS   per Gli Americani

IS IT EXPENSIVE?
    Costa molto?

HOW DO I GET THERE?
    Come ci arrivo?

WOULD YOU WRITE IT DOWN, PLEASE?
    Potrebbe scrivermelo su un pezzo di carta per favore?

DOES ANYONE SPEAK ENGLISH?
    C'è qualcuna che parla inglese?

BUYING, OR NOT

MAY I HELP YOU?
>Ha bisogno d'aiuto?

I HAVE NOT DECIDED.
>Non ho ancora deciso.

I'M JUST BROWSING FOR NOW.
>Sto semplicemente guardando.

IS THAT ALL RIGHT?
>Le da fastidio?

I WILL HELP YOU.
>L' aiuto.

I WON'T BUY ANYTHING, IF YOU PESTER ME.
>Non comprerò niente se non mi lasci sola.

DID YOU MAKE IT?
>L'ha fatto lei?

HOW MUCH DOES THIS COST?
>Quanto costa <u>questo qua?</u>

THAT?   quello la?

HOW MUCH FOR TWO OF THEM?
>Quanto costa per <u>tutte e due?</u>

ALL OF THEM?   tutto quanto?

MAY I TASTE IT?
>Potrei assaggiarlo?

MAY I TRY IT ON?
>Potrei provarlo?

TOO BIG.

    Troppo grande.

TOO SMALL.

    Troppo piccolo.

VERY NICE.

    E molto carino.

IT SUITS YOU EXACTLY.

    Le sta benissimo.

I BET.

    Sono sicura.

I'LL TAKE IT.

    Lo prendo.

I'LL TAKE THEM.

    Li prendo.

I'LL TAKE A KILO.

    Prendo un kilo.

DO YOU ACCEPT TRAVELLERS' CHECKS?

    Accetta "Travellers Cheques"?

    CREDIT CARDS   la carta di credito

    AMERICAN DOLLARS   dollari Americani?

AM I EXPECTED TO BARGAIN?

    Devo mercanteggiare?

IT'S TOO EXPENSIVE FOR ME.

    E troppo caro per me.

I HAVE LITTLE MONEY.

    Ho pochi soldi.

I'M NEARLY BROKE.

    Sono quasi senza soldi.

THE TRUTH IS, I DON'T LIKE IT.

        La verità è che <u>non mi piace</u>

    NEED   non mi serve

    WANT   non lo voglio.

PERHAPS I'LL COME BACK ANOTHER TIME.

    Forse ritornerò un' altra volta.

" IT SUITS YOU EXACTLY. "

EATING OUT

I WOULD LIKE A TABLE FOR ONE.

``Vorrei una tavola per <u>una persona.</u>

TWO	due persone
THREE	tre persone
FOUR	quattro persone.

I WOULD LIKE TODAY'S SPECIALTY.

Vorrei <u>la specialità del giorno.</u>

TODAY'S SOUP	la zuppa del giorno
SOME BREAD	un po' di pane
A VEGETARIAN MEAL.	un pasto vegetariano
SOMETHING LIGHT	qualche cosa di leggero
SOMETHING FILLING	qualcosa che riempia
SOMETHING SPECIAL TO THIS AREA	speciale di questa regione
SOME CHEESE.	del formaggio
SOME WATER	del acqua
SOME FRUIT JUICE	un succo di frutta
A BEER	un birra
A GLASS OF LOCAL WINE	un bicchiere di vino locale
A BOTTLE OF LOCAL WINE.	una bottiglia di vino locale
SOME EGGS.	delle uova
DESSERT	un dolce
A CUP OF COFFEE	un cafè
A CUP OF TEA.	un tazza di tè.

I WANT TO BUY THAT MAN A DRINK.

Voglio offrire qualchecosa da bere <u>a quel signore.</u>

WOMAN	a quella signora.

MAY I GET YOU SOMETHING TO EAT?
    Posso portarle qualchecosa da mangiare?

I AM NOT THIRSTY, THANKS.
    Non ho sete, grazie.

I AM NOT HUNGRY, THANKS.
    Non ho fame, grazie.

WAITER   WAITRESS
    Cameriere   Signorina

THE CHECK, PLEASE.
    Il conto, per favore.

LET ME PAY.
    Pago io.

LET ME PAY FOR MY SHARE.
    Lasciami pagare la mia metà.

ONLY IF YOU INSIST.
    Solo se lei insiste.

I INSIST.
    Insisto.

ARE YOU INSISTENT ABOUT EVERYTHING?
    E insistente su tutto?

TRY ME.
    Provami.
DON'T TRY ME.
    Non mi provocare.

MY COMPLIMENTS TO THE CHEF.
  I miei complimenti al cuoco.

I AM NOT FEELING WELL.
  Non mi sento bene.

WHERE IS THE REST ROOM?
  Dovè è la toilette?

MEN
  Uomini

WOMEN
  Donne

ROCK BOTTOM BUDGET

MAY I CAMP HERE?

    Posso campeggiare qua?

MAY WE CAMP HERE?

    Possaimo campeggiare qua?

            THERE?   là?

I HAVE A SLEEPING BAG.

    Ho un sacco a pelo.

WE HAVE SLEEPING BAGS.

    Abbiamo i nostri sacchi a pelo.

I HAVE A TENT.

    Ho una tenda.

WE HAVE A TENT.

    Abbiamo una tenda.

ARE FIRES PERMISSABLE?

    E permesso accendere un fuoco?

IS THE WATER SAFE?

    L'acqua è potabile?

MAY WE SING IN EXCHANGE FOR A MEAL?

    Posso cantare in cambio d'un pasto?

WOULD YOU ACCEPT THIS IN EXCHANGE FOR A MEAL?

    Accetterebbe questo in cambio d'un pasto?

    A ROOM?   per una stanza?

I AM NOT FOR BARTER.

Non sono in vendita.

WE ARE NOT FOR BARTER.

Non siamo in vendita.

HOW DARE YOU.

Come osi!

THANKS ANYWAY.

Grazie lo stesso.

MISCELLANEOUS ESSENTIALS AND NON-ESSENTIALS

MONEY: Lira

0.	zero
1.	uno
2.	due
4.	quattro
5.	cinque
6.	sei
7.	sette
8.	otto
9.	nove
10.	dieci
11.	undici
12.	dodici
13.	tredici
14.	quattordici
15.	quindici
16.	sedici
17.	diciasette
18.	diociotto
19.	diciannove
20.	venti
21.	ventuno
22.	ventidue
30.	trenta
40.	quaranta
50.	cinquanta
60.	sessanta
70.	settanta
80.	ottanta
90.	novanta
100.	cento

200	duecento
1000	mille
1100	mille cento
2000	due-mila
10,000	dieci-mila
100,000	cento-mila
1,000,000	un millione

WHAT TIME IS IT?
> Che ora è?

NOON.
> Mezzogiorno.

MIDNIGHT.
> Mezzanotte.

ONE O'CLOCK IN THE AFTERNOON
> L'una del pomeriggio

IN THE MORNING.
> L'una di mattina.

TWO O'CLOCK.
> Le due.

TEN PAST TWO
> Le due e dieci.

QUARTER PAST TWO.
> Le due ed un quarto.

HALF PAST TWO
> Le due e mezza.

QUARTER OF TWO.
> Le due meno un quarto.

TEN TO TWO.
> Le due meno dieci.

MAY I SEE YOUR WATCH, PLEASE?
> Posso vedere il suo orologio, per favore?

DAYS, SEASONS, MONTHS & COLORS

SUNDAY	Domenica
MONDAY	Lunedí
TUESDAY	Martedí
WEDNESDAY	Mercoledí
THURSDAY	Giovedí
FRIDAY	Venerdí
SATURDAY	Sabato

SPRING	La primavera
SUMMER	L'estate
FALL	L'autunno
WINTER	L'inverno

JANUARY	Gennaio	RED	rosso
FEBRUARY	Febbraio	ORANGE	arancione
MARCH	Marzo	YELLOW	giallo
APRIL	Aprile	GREEN	verde
MAY	Maggio	BLUE	blù
JUNE	Giugno	PURPLE	viola
JULY	Luglio	PINK	rosa
AUGUST	Agosto	BROWN	marrone
SEPTEMBER	Settembre	BEIGE	beige
OCTOBER	Ottobre	GREY	grigio
NOVEMBER	Novembre	BLACK	nero
DECEMBER	Dicembre	WHITE	bianco

COME ONS AND TURN OFFS

HAVEN'T WE MET BEFORE?

    Non ci conosciamo?

WHAT'S A MAN LIKE YOU DOING IN A PLACE LIKE THIS?

    Che cosa fa un uomo della sua classe in un posto come questo?

ARE YOU WAITING FOR SOMEONE?

    Aspetta qualcuno?

IS THIS YOUR FIRST TRIP TO _____?

    E il suo primo viaggio a_____?

ARE YOU ENJOYING IT?

    Lei si sta divertendo?

        HAVE YOU VISITED _____?

        Lei ha visitato_____?

WHAT A PITY!

    Che peccato!

DO YOU LIKE THE _____PEOPLE?

    Lei trova la gente _____simpatica?

MAY I SIT WITH YOU?

        Posso sedermi vicino a Lei?

    BE YOUR GUIDE?   essere la sua guida?

    TAKE YOU DANCING?   portarla a ballare?

    TAKE YOU FOR A WALK IN THE MOONLIGHT?

    le piacerebbe camminare nella luce della luna?

    SHOW YOU WHERE I LIVE?   farle vedere dove abito?

YOU AMERICAN WOMEN ARE SO FORWARD.

    Loro donne Americane sono così emancipate.

YES.

    Sì.

NO.

    No.

HARDLY.   I"D LIKE THAT.

    Non mi piacerebbe.   Mi piacerebbe.

I DO NOT SPEAK ITALIAN.

    Non parlo italiano.

I WISH TO BE ALONE.

    Desidero essere lasciata da sola.

I AM TRYING TO THINK.

                Sto cercando di <u>pensare</u>.

    READ   leggere

    SLEEP   dormire.

I PREFER MY OWN COMPANY, IF YOU DON'T MIND.

    Preferisco essere da sola per favore.

PLEASE DO NOT DISTURB ME.

    Per favore, non disturbarmi.

I HAVE AN EXTREMELY CONTAGIOUS DISEASE.

    Soffro di una malatia estremamente contagiosa.

WHAT IS YOUR NAME?

Come si chiama?

MY NAME IS_____.
    Mi chiamo_____.

HOW VERY AMERICAN.
           Quello è tipicamente <u>americano</u>!

FRENCH	francese
GERMAN	tedesco.
ITALIAN	italiano
SPANISH	spagnolo

WHERE ARE YOU FROM?
    Da dove viene lei?

I AM FROM THE UNITED STATES.
        Vengo <u>dall' America.</u>
    EAST OF THE SUN AND WEST OF THE MOON
           da est del sole ed ovest della luna
    A SMALL TOWN
           da un piccolo villagio.

WHAT INTERESTS YOU IN LIFE?
    Che cosa Le interessa nella vita?

WHAT ARE YOU SEEKING?
        Che cosa cercha lei?

AN ECSTATIC MOMENT	un momento estatico
ART	arte
ASTROLOGY	astrologia
BUSINESS	commercio
COOKING	la cucina
CONTRADICTIONS	contradizioni
DANCING	ballare

DREAMS	i sogni
ECOLOGY	l'ecologia.
EXCITEMENT	l'avventura
EXERCISE	l'esercizio
FEMINISM	il femminismo
FILM	Il cinema
GETTING HOME SAFELY	
	ritornare a casa senza alcuno pericolo
HAPPINESS	la felicità
INCONSEQUENTIAL MATTERS, TO YOU, PROBABLY	
	probabilmente, cose di nessuna importanza
	per lei.
LIBERAL CAUSES	le cause liberali
LIFE, LIBERTY, AND THE PURSUIT OF HAPPINESS	
	la vita, la libertà e la ricerca della felicità
MONEY	il denaro
MUSIC	la musica
NOTHING MUCH	niente di speciale
POETRY	la poesia
POLITICS	la politica
POWER	il potere
QUIET	la tranquillità
READING	la letteratura
RELIGION	la religione
SAVING THE WORLD	salvare il mondo
SEX	il sesso
SPORTS	lo sport
THE PERFECT WAVE	l'onda perfetta.
THE THEATER	il teatro
THEATRICS	il dramma
TRUTH	la veritá
VAGARIES OF THE UNIVERSE	I capricci del universo
YOU	lei.

FASCINATING!

Affascinante!

I DO NOT BELIEVE IT.

Non è vero!

WHAT ASTROLOGICAL SIGN ARE YOU?

Di che segno è Lei?

WHAT IS YOUR RISING SIGN?

Di che segno ascendente è Lei?

AQUARIUS	Acquario
PISCES	Pesce
ARIES	Ariete
TAURUS	Toro
GEMINI	Gemelli
CANCER	Cancro
LEO	Leone
VIRGO	Vergine
LIBRA	Bilancia
SCORPIO	Scorpione
SAGITARRIUS	Sagittario
CAPRICORN	Capricorno

I DON'T KNOW WHAT YOU'RE TALKING ABOUT.

Non capisco di che cosa lei sta parlando.

WHAT KIND OF WOMAN DO YOU ENJOY?

Che tipo di donna ti piace?

I AM MORE INTERESTED IN INTELLIGENCE

Sono piu interessata nella intelligenza

CHARM	nella graziosità
HUMOR	nel senso dell' umori
SEX	nel sesso,

THAN I AM IN CHARM...

        che <u>nella graziosità...</u>

HUMOR	senso dell' umori
SEX	sesso
INTELLIGENCE.	intelligenza.

ARE YOU TRYING TO GET OVER A ROMANCE?

    Lei sta cercando di dimenticare una relazione passata?

I AM TRYING TO GET OVER A ROMANCE.

    Sto provando a dimenticare una relazione passata.

HOW ROMANTIC.

    `E molto romantico.

I AM NOT ROMANTIC.

    Non sono romantica.

ARE YOU MARRIED?

    Lei è sposato? *to a man*

        sposata? *to a woman*

I AM MARRIED.

    Sono sposata.

        I AM NOT MARRIED.

            Non sono sposata.

SORT OF.

    In un certo modo, sì.

FORTUNATELY, NO.

    Fortunatamente, no.

UNFORTUNATELY, NO.

    Sfortunatamente, no.

I AM SINGLE...

Sono nubile *fem.*   scapolo *masc.*

...BUT LIVING WITH SOMEONE

...però vivo con qualcuno.

I AM SEPARATED.

Sono separata

DIVORCED   divorziata

WIDOWED   vedova.

DO YOU HAVE ANY CHILDREN?

Lei ha dei figli?

FORTUNATELY, NO.

Fortunatamente, no.

UNFORTUNATELY, NO.

Sfortunatamente, no.

I HAVE ONE CHILD.

Ho una figlia *fem.*   un figlio *masc.*

TWO   due figli

THREE   tre figli

MANY CHILDREN.   tanti figli.

ARE YOU HOMOSEXUAL?

Lei è omosessuale?

I AM HOMOSEXUAL.

Sono omosessuale.

I AM NOT HOMOSEXUAL.

Non sono omosessuale.

I MIGHT BECOME HOMOSEXUAL SOON.
   Forse diventerò omosessuale presto.

IT IS NONE OF YOUR BUSINESS.
   Non sono affari suoi.

GUESS.
   Indovini.

DO YOU CONSIDER YOURSELF A FEMINIST?   A SEXIST?
   Si considera una femminista?   un maschilista?

WOULD YOU LIKE TO DISCUSS IT?
   Le piacerebbe discuterne?

IS THERE A FEMINIST ORGANIZATION HERE?
   C'è una organizzazione femminista qua vicino?

IS IT POSSIBLE TO MEET SOME FEMINIST WOMEN?
   `E possible incontrare delle donne femministe?
              MEN?   incontrar degli uomini femministI?

DO YOU THINK THAT MEN AND WOMEN SHOULD BE EDUCATED THE
SAME?
   Lei crede che l'educazione dovrebbe essere lo stesso per
                               tutte e due i sessi?
   PAID THE SAME?
          Lei crede che la paga dovrebbe...
   TREATED THE SAME?
          Lei crede che il trattamento dovrebbe...
WHY NOT?
   Perchè no?
OF COURSE!
   Certamente!

THAT IS CONTRARY TO THE LAWS OF NATURE.

E contrario alla legge della natura.

YOU LOOK BEAUTIFUL WHEN YOU'RE ANGRY.

Lei è molto attraente quando è` arrabbiato. *to a man.*

bella quando è arrabbiata. *to a woman.*

IT SEEMS WE HAVE LITTLE IN COMMON.

Sembra che non abbiamo niente in comune.

IT SEEMS WE HAVE MUCH IN COMMON.

Sembra che abbiamo tanto in comune.

IN YOUR COUNTRY, ARE MOST MEN LIKE YOU?

In suo paese, la maggior parte degli uomini sono come lei?

IN MY COUNTRY, MOST WOMEN ARE LIKE ME.

Si, la maggior parte delle donne sono come me.

SHALL WE SEE EACH OTHER AGAIN?

Ci rincontriamo un' altra volta?

WHAT A RIDICULOUS IDEA!

Che idea stupida!

HOPELESS!	ridicola!
HORRIBLE!	orribile!
INSPIRED!	brilliante!

WHERE SHALL WE MEET?

Dove ci incontriamo?

AT MY PLACE	A casa mia.
YOUR PLACE	A casa sua
A LARGE CAFE	In un grande caffé
IN PUBLIC	In un luogo pubblico

SOMEWHERE WHERE WE CAN BE ALONE
In un posto dove possiamo essere soli

A DIVE   un locale malfamato

SOMEWHERE REDOLENT OF UNRESTRAINED PASSION &
INTRIGUE
locale suggestivo di passione ed imbroglio incontrolabile

A PLACE WITH LIVE MUSIC   locale dove si suona musica

A RESTAURANT FAVORED BY WEAK-STOMACHED TOURISTS
ristorante per i turisti con stomachi delicati

A PLACE WHERE YOU'D TAKE YOUR PARENTS
posto dove si potrebbero portare i suoi genitori

ANYWHERE WITH A VIEW   posto con una bella vista.

PERHAPS YOU CAN SURPRISE ME?
Perchè non mi fa una sorpresa?

LET ME SURPRISE YOU.
Perchè non Le faccio una sorpresa.

I BEG YOUR PARDON.
Le chiedo le mie scuse.

WHEN SHALL WE MEET?
Quando ci rivediamo?

THE EARLIER THE BETTER
Al più presto possibile.

THE LATER THE BETTER.

    Al più tardi possibile.

SHALL I BRING A CHAPERONE?

    Devo portare qualcuno che mi accompagni?

YOU ARE TOO FUNNY.

    Lei è così divertente.

I'VE ALWAYS DEPENDED UPON THE KINDNESS OF STRANGERS.

    Ricorro sempre alla gentilezza della gente.

IS THAT FROM A PLAY?

    L'ha preso da un pezzo di teatro?

THAT IS FROM A PLAY.

    E da un pezzo di teatro.

YOU ARE TOO CLEVER.

    Lei è proprio furbo *to a man*

            furba *to a woman.*

GOODBYE FOR NOW.

    Ciao per adesso.

SLEEPING ARRANGEMENTS

IS THERE A CHEAP HOTEL NEARBY?

                C'è <u>un albergo che non costi molto qua vicino?</u>

    CLEAN   un albergo pulito qua vicino

    GOOD   un buon albergo qua vicino?

WHERE IS THE NEAREST YOUTH HOSTEL?

    Dov'è il più vicino ostello della gioventù?

DO YOU KNOW WHERE I COULD RENT A ROOM?

    Lei sa dove <u>posso</u> affittare una stanza?

    WE   possiamo

FOR HOW MANY DAYS?

    Per quanti giorni?

JUST FOR TONIGHT.

                Solamente <u>per una notte</u>.

    FOR A WEEK   per una settimana

    FOR A MONTH.   per un mese.

HOW MUCH DOES THE ROOM COST PER NIGHT?

    Quanto costa la stanza per una notte?

IS IT QUIET?

    La stanza è tranquilla?

DOES IT HAVE A NICE VIEW?

    Ha una bella vista?

I'D LIKE SOMETHING THAT EVOKES THE ROMANCE OF AGES PAST.

    Mi piacerebbe qualchecosa che rievoca il carattere dei

               giorni passati.

I HAVE JUST THE ROOM FOR YOU.

    Ho la stanza adatta.

I'M SORRY; WE HAVE MODERNIZED.

    Scusate, ma abbiamo modernizato tutto quanto.

I WANT A PRIVATE BATH.

    Voglio un bagno privato.

I DO NOT WANT A PRIVATE BATH.

    Non ho bisogno di un bagno privato.

WE WOULD LIKE A DOUBLE BED.

    Vogliamo un letto matrimoniale.

WE WOULD LIKE TWIN BEDS.

    Vogliamo due letti separati.

IS BREAKFAST INCLUDED?

    La prima colazione è inclusa?

MAY I SEE THE ROOM PLEASE?

    <u>Potrei</u> vedere la stanza per favore?

WE   Possiamo

HAVE YOU ANY OTHERS?

    Avete altre stanze?

THANK YOU FOR YOUR TROUBLE.

    Grazie per il suo disturbo.

FINE, I'LL TAKE IT.

    Bene, lo voglio.

WE'LL TAKE IT.

    Bene, lo vogliamo.

WHEN IS CHECK OUT TIME?

    A che ora dobbiamo vacare la stanza?

I WOULD LIKE SOME SOAP.

                          Vorrei <u>del sapone.</u>

SOME TOWELS	degli asciugamani
SOME DRINKING WATER	dell' acqua potabile
A BLANKET	una coperta.
SOME QUIET.	silenzio e tranquillità.

THE KEY TO ROOM _____, PLEASE.

    La chiave della stanza numero _____per favore.

ARE THERE ANY MESSAGES FOR ME?

    Ci sono dei messaggi per me?

I AM EXPECTING A VISITOR.

    Aspetto delle visite.

COME IN.

    Avanti!

INTIMACIES

HOW GOOD TO SEE YOU.
> Che piacere rivederti.

MY DEAR.
> Mio caro *to a man*
>> mia cara *to a woman.*

HOW ARE YOU?
> Come stai?

I AM WONDERFUL.

	Mi sento <u>fantastica</u>!
TERRIBLE	terribile
NERVOUS	nervosa
EAGER	eccitata
TIRED	stanca.

I AM AS YOU SEE.
> Sono come mi vedi.

I AM TIRED, BUT NOT TOO TIRED.
> Sono stanca, ma non troppo.

I AM BUT PUTTY IN YOUR HANDS
> Mi liquefaccio nelle tue mani.

A SHADOW OF MY FORMER SELF.
> Sono l'ombra di quello che ero.

LET ME BE THE JUDGE OF THAT.
> Lasciami giudicare da me.

YOU FOOL.
> Idiota!

DO YOU MIND IF I LOCK THE DOOR?

Ti da fastidio se chiudo a chiave la porta?

PULL THE CURTAINS CLOSED	tiro le tende
PULL THE CURTAINS OPEN	apro le tende
SEND THE SERVANTS AWAY	mando via i domestici
MAKE MYSELF COMFORTABLE?	mi metto comoda?
DOUSE THE INCENSE	spengo l'incenso
TURN DOWN THE VOLUME	abbasso il volume
TURN UP THE VOLUME	also il volume
RECONSIDER	o riconsidero
INTRODUCE YOU TO A FRIEND	

...ti presento a una amica *fem.*

un amico *masc.*

SHALL WE UNDRESS?

Ci spogliamo?

SHALL WE NOT UNDRESS?

Non ci spogliamo, allora?

LET'S NOT HURRY.

Non ci affrettiamo.

LET'S NOT WASTE TIME.

Non perdiamo tempo.

ARE YOU CLEAN?

Hai delle malattie?

DO YOU KNOW WHAT I MEAN?

Sai che voglio dire?

ARE YOU SURE?

Sei certo? *to a man*   Sei certa? *to a woman.*

I CONSIDER THAT AN INSULT.

Lo prendo come un insulto.

I'M SURE YOU DO.

Sono sicura che lo prendi in quel modo.

I LOVE YOUR EYES.

Amo i tuoi occhi.

HAIR	i tuoi capelli
MOUTH	la tua bocca
TONGUE	la tua lingua
FACE	il tuo viso
RIGHT SHOULDER	la tua spalla destra
SKIN	la tua pelle
FEET	i tuoi piedi
IMPERFECTIONS	le tue imperfezioni
STOMACH	il tuo stomaco
SMELL	il tuo odore
UNDERWEAR	le tue mutande
ENERGY	la tua energia
PERSISTANCE	la tua persistenza.

I LOVE YOU.

Ti amo.

I LOVE YOU, BUT I DON'T LIKE YOU.

Ti amo ma non mi piaci.

I LIKE YOU, BUT I DON'T LOVE YOU.

Mi piaci ma non ti amo.

YOUR KISSES ARE DIVINE.

I tuoi baci sono divini.

UNUSUAL   sono originali.

THIS IS MY FIRST TIME.

Questa è la prima volta per me.

IS THIS YOUR FIRST TIME?

E la prima volta per te?

I CONSIDER THAT AN INSULT.

Lo considero come un insulto.

HAVE YOU CHANGED YOUR MIND?

Hai cambiato idea?

.

NOT EXACTLY.

Non esattamente.

I HAVE CHANGED MY MIND.

Ho cambiato idea.

PERHAPS WE CAN BE FRIENDS.

Forse potremo essere amici.

I MUST MAKE CERTAIN I WILL NOT GET PREGNANT.

Devo prendere precauzioni per non restare incinta.

I DIDN'T MEAN THAT.

Non volevo intenderlo.

AM I HURTING YOU?

Ti faccio male?

YES.

Sì.

NO.

No.

A LITTLE.

    Un po'.

SURELY YOU JEST.

    Sicuramente ti diverti.

WE ARE LIKE TWO SHIPS PASSING IN THE NIGHT.

    Siamo come <u>due navi che si incrociano nella notte.</u>

    A PAIR OF LOVE BIRDS   due passerotti

        innamorati

    A SYMPHONY OF THE SENSES   un' impero dei sensi

    A BAD MOVIE   un brutto film.

HOW ORIGINAL!

    Che originale!

WHY ARE YOU READING FROM THE LITTLE BOOK?

    Perche leggi da quel piccolo libro?

DO YOU LIKE THIS?

    Questo ti piace?

WHAT?

    Che cosa?

I DO NOT LIKE THAT.

    Quello non mi piace.

I LIKE THAT.

    Quello mi piace.

ONE MORE TIME.

    Ancora un' altra volta.

LET ME DO THAT.

    Lasciamelo fare.

WHAT ABOUT ME?

 Ed io allora?

I FORGOT.

 Mi sono dimenticata *fem.*

  dimenticato *masc.*

PATIENCE IS A VIRTUE.

 La pazienza è una virtù.

HOW EXQUISITE!

 Che squisito!

IT DOESN'T MATTER.

 Non fa niente.

MY DEAR.

 Mio caro *to a man*

  mia cara *to a woman*

THAT TICKLES.

 Oh, che solletico!

I'M NOT LAUGHING AT YOU.

 Non sto ridendo di te.

THERE IS NO BETTER PLACE TO LAUGH THAN IN BED.

 Non c'è migliore posto per ridere che in letto.

WHAT IS SO FUNNY?

 Che cosa cè di così divertente?

EVERYTHING / NOTHING.

 Tutto / Niente.

THAT WAS MY FIRST TIME.

    Era la prima volta per me.

WAS THAT YOUR FIRST TIME?

    Era la prima volta per te?

I FIND THAT DIFFICULT TO BELIEVE.

    Lo trovo difficile da credere.

LET'S GO TO SLEEP.

    Andiamo a dormire.

        LET'S NOT GO TO SLEEP.

            Non andiamo a dormire.

IT'S A PITY WE DON'T SPEAK THE SAME LANGUAGE.

    E un peccato che non parliamo la stessa lingua.

I'M GLAD WE SPEAK THE SAME LANGUAGE.

    Son felice che parliamo la stessa lingua.

ARE YOU TIRED?

    Sei stanco *to a man*

        sei stanca? *to a woman.*

I AM TIRED.

    Sono stanca.

I NEVER TIRE.

    Non mi stanco mai.

GOOD MORNING.

    Buon giorno!

SPANISH

" I'VE CHANGED MY MIND."

BASIC CHAT:

YES	Si
NO	No
PLEASE	Por favor
THANKS	Gracias
HELLO	Hola

Hints on pronunciation:

The same vowels appear in both Spanish and English; you will see accents occasionally over the a, the e, and the i, as well as ñ.

a	ah as in *shah*
e	a as in *say*
i	ee as in *teeth*
o	oh as in *soap*
u	oo as in *tool*
eu	weh as in *away*

The consonants are rather as they are in English, except that h is never pronounced, the r is trilled, and n written as ñ is pronounced ny, as in nyah nyah.

ca, co and cu	cah as in *caught*
ce and ci	seh as in *send* (Mexico)
	th as in *that* (Spain)
ga, go and gu	guh as in *get*
ge and gi	hach as in *happy*
h	silent
j	choh as in san *josé*
ll	iyll as in *million*
ñ	ny as in *canyon*
r	trilled
z	s as in *soft* (Mexico)
	th as in *that* (Spain)

ON THE STREET

GOOD DAY.
>Buenos días.

GOOD AFTERNOON.
>Buenas tardes.

GOOD EVENING.
>Buenas noches.

SAME TO YOU.
>Igualmente.

I'M NOT INTERESTED.
>No me interesa.

IN THAT, EITHER.
>Ni eso tampoco.

STOP FOLLOWING ME.
>No me siga.

GET AWAY!
>¡Váyase!

PLEASE.
>Por favor.

YOU ARE AN INSULT TO YOUR COUNTRY.
>Usted es un insulto <u>a su patria.</u>

CITY	a su ciudad.
VILLAGE	a su aldea
MOTHER	a su madre.

LEAVE ME ALONE, YOU ANIMAL.
>¡Déjeme en paz, <u>bruto.</u>

| PIG | marrano |
| IMBECILE | imbécil! |

IF YOU DON'T STOP

Si no <u>se detiene usted</u>

MOVE se mueve usted

BEHAVE LIKE A GENTLEMAN, se porta usted como caballero,

I'LL CALL THE POLICE.

llamaré a la policía.

HELP!

¡Socorro!

POLICE!

¡Policía!

I HOPE I DIDN'T HURT YOU TOO BADLY.

Espero que yo no lo haya lastimado demasiado.

EXCUSE ME.

Perdóneme.

"IMBECILE."

AROUND TOWN

WHERE AM I?
>¿Dónde estoy?

WHERE IS THE BUS STATION?
>¿Dónde está <u>la estación de autobús?</u>

SUBWAY	el metro
TRAIN STATION	la estación de trenes
AIRPORT	el aeropuerto?

MAY I GET OUT HERE?
>¿Puedo bajar aquí?

HOW DO I GET TO_____?
>¿Cómo se llega a __?

WHERE MAY I RENT A CAR?
>¿Dónde puedo alquilar un coche?

WHERE IS A GAS STATION?
>¿Dónde está una gasolinera?

FILL IT UP, PLEASE.
>Llénelo, por favor

WITH SUPER	con super
WITH REGULAR	con gasolina regular
WITH DIESEL	con diesel.

WHERE IS A PUBLIC BATH
>¿Dónde hay <u>un baño público</u>?

| TOILET | un retrete? |

WHERE IS THE MARKET?
>¿Dónde hay un mercado?

WHEN DOES IT OPEN?
>¿A qué hora abre?

WHERE IS A BOOKSTORE

       ¿Dónde hay una librería?

TRAVEL BUREAU	una agencia de viajes
BANK	un banco
POST OFFICE	una oficina de correos?

AIRMAIL STAMPS, PLEASE.

    Estampillas de correo aéreo, por favor.

WHERE MAY I MAKE A LOCAL TELEPHONE CALL?

      ¿Dónde puedo hacer una llamada local?

| LONG DISTANCE? | una llamada de larga distancia? |

DO YOU KNOW WHERE THE AMERICAN EMBASSY IS?

    ¿Puede usted decirme dónde está la Embajada
                                 de los Estados Unidos?

CONSULATE	el Consulado
EXPRESS OFFICE	la oficina de American Espress
A HOSPITAL	un hospital
A DOCTOR...	un médico...
... WHO SPEAKS ENGLISH	... que hable inglés
A DRUGSTORE	una farmacia?

DO YOU SELL ANYTHING FOR HEADACHES

      ¿Se vende algo para un dolor de cabeza?

DIARRHEA	la diarrea
CONSTIPATION	el estreñimiento
SUNBURN	las quemaduras de sol?

DO YOU SELL SOAP?

      ¿Se vende aquí jabón?

SHAMPOO	champú
DEODORANT	desodorante
DIAPHRAGM CREAM	crema para diafragmas

CONDOMS	anticonceptivos
TAMPONS	tampón
SANITARY NAPKINS	toallas higiénicas
TOOTHPASTE	pasta dentífrica
TOOTHBRUSHES	cepillos de dientes
TALCUM POWDER	talco
SUNTAN LOTION	aceite bronceador

WHERE MIGHT I FIND A GYM?

¿Puede usted decirme dónde hay <u>un gimnasio</u>?

BEAUTY PARLOR	un salón de belleza
FORTUNE TELLER	un adivino
MASSEUSE	una masajista
MOVIE THEATER	un cine
THEATER	un teatro
MUSIC	un lugar donde se toca música
A PLACE TO DANCE	un lugar donde se baila
A POOL HALL	una sala de billar
VIDEO GAMES ARCADE	un lugar con juegos de video

GOOD, CHEAP, UNDERRATED RESTAURANT

un buen restaurante barato y desconocido

RESTAURANT UNKNOWN TO TOURISTS?

un restaurante desconocido por turistas?

WHERE IS THE ACTION AT NIGHT?

¿Dónde se puede divertirse por la noche?

IS IT SAFE FOR A WOMAN BY HERSELF?

¿Puede salir sin <u>miedo una mujer sola</u>?

FOR WOMEN?	miedo las mujeres solas?
FOR AMERICANS?	norteamericanos?

IS IT EXPENSIVE?

¿Es cara *fem*   caro ? *masc.*

HOW DO I GET THERE?

¿Cómo se llega allá?

WOULD YOU WRITE IT DOWN, PLEASE?

Por favor escríbalo.

DOES ANYONE SPEAK ENGLISH?

¿Hay alguien que hable inglés?

BUYING, OR NOT

MAY I HELP YOU?
    ¿En que puedo servirle?

I HAVE NOT DECIDED.
    No he decidido todavía.

I'M JUST BROWSING FOR NOW.
    Estoy sólo mirando por el momento.

IS THAT ALL RIGHT?
    ¿Está bien?

I WILL HELP YOU.
    Voy a ayudarle.

I WON'T BUY ANYTHING, IF YOU PESTER ME.
    No compraré nada si usted me molesta.

DID YOU MAKE IT?
    ¿Lo hizo usted?

DID YOU GROW IT?
    ¿Lo cultivó usted?

HOW MUCH DOES THIS COST?
    ¿Cuánto cuesta <u>esto</u>?
       THAT   eso?

HOW MUCH FOR TWO OF THEM?
    ¿Cuánto cuestan <u>los dos?</u>
       ALL OF THEM?   todos?

MAY I TASTE IT?

    ¿Me permite <u>probarla</u>?

    TRY IT ON?   probármelo *masc.*

                  probármela *fem.*

TOO BIG.

    Es demasiado <u>grande.</u>

    SMALL   pequeña.

VERY NICE.

    Es muy <u>bonito.</u>   *masc.*

           bonita.   *f em.*

IT SUITS YOU EXACTLY.

    Le queda muy bien.

I BET.

   ¡No me diga!

I'LL TAKE IT.   I'LL TAKE THEM.

    Me lo llevo.   Me los llevo.

I'LL TAKE A KILO.

    Quiero un kilo.

DO YOU ACCEPT TRAVELLERS' CHECKS?

              ¿Acepta usted <u>cheques de viajero?</u>

    CREDIT CARDS   tarjetas de crédito?

    U.S. DOLLARS   dólares?

AM I EXPECTED TO BARGAIN?

    ¿Es necesario regatear?

IT'S TOO EXPENSIVE FOR ME.

    Es demasiado cara.

I HAVE LITTLE MONEY.

    Tengo poco dinero.

I'M NEARLY BROKE.

    Estoy casi sin plata.

THE TRUTH IS, I DON'T LIKE IT.

                            La verdad es que <u>no me gusta</u>.

    NEED   no la necesito.

    DON'T WANT IT.   no la quiero.

PERHAPS I'LL COME BACK ANOTHER TIME.

    Tal vez volveré otro día.

EATING OUT

I WOULD LIKE A TABLE FOR ONE, PLEASE.

Quisiera una mesa para <u>una persona</u>, por favor.

TWO	dos personas
THREE	tres personas
FOUR	quatro personas.

I WOULD LIKE TODAY'S SPECIALTY.

Yo quisiera <u>el plato del día.</u>

TODAY'S SOUP	la sopa del día
BREAD	pan
A VEGETARIAN MEAL	una comida vegetariana
SOMETHING LIGHT	comer algo ligero
SOMETHING FILLING	comer algo substancial
SOMETHING SPECIAL TO THIS AREA	

comer alguna expecialidad de esta región

SOME CHEESE	queso
SOME WATER	un vaso de agua
SOME FRUIT JUICE	un jugo de fruta.
A BEER	una cerveza
A GLASS OF LOCAL WINE	una copa de vino de la región
A BOTTLE OF LOCAL WINE	una botella de vino de la región
SOME EGGS	unos huevos
DESSERT	un postre
A CUP OF COFFEE	un taza de café
A CUP OF TEA	una taza de té.

I WANT TO BUY THAT MAN A DRINK.

Yo quisiera ofrecerle una copa a <u>ese señor</u>.

THAT WOMAN	esa señora.

MAY I GET YOU SOMETHING TO EAT?
   ¿Quiere usted comer algo?

I AM NOT THIRSTY, THANKS.
   No tengo sed, gracias.

I AM NOT HUNGRY, THANKS.
   No tengo hambre, gracias.

WAITER   WAITRESS
   mesero   mesera
THE CHECK, PLEASE.
   La cuenta, por favor.

LET ME PAY.
    Permítame pagar.

LET ME PAY FOR MY SHARE.
   Permítame pagar lo mío.

ONLY IF YOU INSIST.
   Solamente si usted insiste.

I INSIST.
    Si, yo insisto.

ARE YOU INSISTENT ABOUT EVERYTHING?
   ¿Insiste usted en todo?

TRY ME.
   ¿Quiere usted probarme?

DON'T TRY ME.
   No me tiente usted.

MY COMPLIMENTS TO THE CHEF.

Mis felicitaciones al cocinero.

I AM NOT FEELING WELL.

No me siento bien.

WHERE IS THE REST ROOM?

¿Dónde están los servicios? *for Spain*

¿Dónde está el baño? *for Mexico*

MEN

Caballeros

WOMEN

Damas

ROCK BOTTOM BUDGET

MAY I CAMP HERE?

    ¿Puedo acampar <u>aquí?</u>

       THERE?   allí?

MAY WE CAMP HERE?

    ¿Podemos acampar aquí?

I HAVE A SLEEPING BAG.

       <u>Tengo un saco</u> de dormir.

WE HAVE...   Tenemos sacos...

I HAVE A TENT.

    Tengo una tienda de campaña.

ARE FIRES PERMISSABLE?

    ¿Se permite encender una hoguera?

IS THE WATER SAFE TO DRINK?

    ¿Hay agua potable?

MAY I SING IN EXCHANGE FOR A MEAL?

    <u>¿Puedo cantar</u> a cambio de una comida ?

    MAY WE SING...

       ¿Podemos cantar...

WOULD YOU ACCEPT THIS IN EXCHANGE FOR A MEAL?

    ¿Podría usted aceptar esto a cambio de <u>una comida</u>?

I AM NOT FOR BARTER.

    No me vendo.

WE ARE NOT FOR BARTER

    No nos vendemos.

HOW DARE YOU.

    ¿Cómo se atreve usted?

THANKS ANYWAY.

    Gracias de todos modos.

MISCELLANEOUS ESSENTIALS AND NON-ESSENTIALS

| | MONEY: | Spain | La peseta |
| | | Mexico | El peso |

0.	cero
1.	uno
2.	dos
3.	tres
4.	cuatro
5.	cinco
6.	seis
7.	siete
8.	ocho
9.	nueve
10.	diez
11.	once
12.	doce
13.	trece
14.	catorce
15.	quince
16.	dieciseis
17.	diecisiete
18.	dieciocho
19.	diecinueve
20.	viente
21.	viente y uno
22.	viente y dox
30.	treinta
40.	cuarenta
50.	cincuenta
60.	sesenta
70.	setenta
80.	ochenta
90.	noventa
100.	cien
200.	dos cientos
1000.	mil

1100.	mil cien
2000.	dos mil
10,000.	diez mil
100,000.	cien mil
1,000,000.	un millón

WHAT TIME IS IT?
>¿Qué hora es?

NOON.
>Mediodía.

MIDNIGHT.
>Medianoche.

ONE O'CLOCK IN THE AFTERNOON
>La una <u>de la tarde</u>

IN THE MORNING.
>de la mañana.

TWO O'CLOCK.
>Las dos.

TEN PAST TWO	QUARTER PAST TWO
Las dos y diez	las dos y cuarto

HALF PAST TWO	QUARTER OF TWO.
Las dos y media	las dos menos cuarto.

TEN TO TWO.
>Las dos menos diez.

MAY I SEE YOUR WATCH, PLEASE?
>¿Me permite usted ver su reloj?

DAYS, SEASONS , MONTHS & COLORS

SUNDAY	Domingo		
MONDAY	Lunes	SPRING	La primavera
TUESDAY	Martes		
WEDNESDAY	Miércoles	SUMMER	El verano
THURSDAY	Jueves		
FRIDAY	Viernes	FALL	El otoño
SATURDAY	Sábado		
		WINTER	El invierno

JANUARY	Enero
FEBRUARY	Febrero
MARCH	Marzo
APRIL	Abril
MAY	Mayo
JUNE	Junio
JULY	Julio
AUGUST	Agosto
SEPTEMBER	Septiembre
OCTOBER	Octubre
NOVEMBER	Novembre
DECEMBER	Diciembre

	feminine	*masculine*
RED	roja	rojo
ORANGE	naranjada	naranjado
YELLOW	amarilla	amarillo
GREEN	verde	
BLUE	azul	
PURPLE	purpúreo	
PINK	rosa	
BROWN	café	
BEIGE	beige	
GREY	gris	
BLACK	negra	negro
WHITE	blanca	blanco

COME ONS AND TURN OFFS

HAVEN'T WE MET BEFORE?
>   ¿No nos hemos conocido antes?

WHAT'S A MAN   LIKE YOU DOING IN A PLACE LIKE THIS?
>   ¿Qué hace aquí un hombre como usted?
>   WOMAN   una mujer

ARE YOU WAITING FOR SOMEONE?
>   ¿Espera usted a alguien?

IS THIS YOUR FIRST TRIP TO _____?
>   ¿Es su primer viaje a _____?

ARE YOU ENJOYING IT?   HAVE YOU VISITED_____?
>   ¿Se divierte usted?   ¿Ha visitado usted _____?

WHAT A PITY!
>   ¡Qué lástima!

DO YOU LIKE THE SPANISH PEOPLE?
>   ¿Son simpáticos los españoles?
>   AMERICANS   norteamericanas
>   MEXICANS   mexicanos

MAY I SIT WITH YOU?
>   Puedo sentarme aquí?
>   BE YOUR GUIDE   servirle de guía
>   TAKE YOU DANCING
>   invitarla *fem.* invitarlo *masc.* a bailar
>   TAKE YOU FOR A WALK IN THE MOONLIGHT
>   invitarla *fem.* a dar un paseo a la luz de la luna?
>   invitarlo *masc.*
>   SHOW YOU WHERE I LIVE?   mostrarle el lugar donde vivo?

YOU AMERICAN WOMEN ARE SO FORWARD.

¡Ustedes las norteamericanas son tan atrevidas!

YES.

Sí.

NO.

No.

I'D LIKE THAT.   HARDLY.

Me gustaría eso.   No me gustaría eso.

I DO NOT SPEAK SPANISH.

Yo no hablo español.

I WISH TO BE ALONE.

Quiero estar sola.

I AM TRYING TO THINK .

Estoy tratando de pensar.

READ   leer

SLEEP   dormir

I PREFER MY OWN COMPANY, IF YOU DON'T MIND.

Prefiero estar sola, si no le molesta a usted.

PLEASE DO NOT DISTURB ME.

Por favor, déjeme en paz.

I HAVE AN EXTREMELY CONTAGIOUS DISEASE.

Padezco de una enfermedad muy contagiosa.

WHAT IS YOUR NAME?

¿Cómo se llama usted?

MY NAME IS____.

  Me llamo____.

HOW VERY AMERICAN.

          ¡Eso es tipicamente <u>norteamericano</u>!

  FRENCH   francés

  GERMAN   alemán

  ITALIAN   italiano

  SPANISH   español

WHERE ARE YOU FROM?

  ¿De dónde es usted?

I AM FROM THE UNITED STATES.

  Soy de los Estados Unidos.

  EAST OF THE SUN AND WEST OF THE MOON.

          Vengo del este del sol y del oeste de la luna.

  I AM FROM A SMALL TOWN.

          Vengo de un pueblito.

WHAT INTERESTS YOU IN LIFE?

  ¿Qué le interesa a usted en la vida?

WHAT ARE YOU SEEKING?

          ¿Qué busca usted?

  AN ECSTATIC MOMENT   un momento de éxtasis

  ART   el arte

  ASTROLOGY   la astrología

  BUSINESS   los negocios

  COOKING   la cocina

  CONTRADICTIONS   las contradicciones

  DANCING   el baile

  DREAMS   los sueños

  ECOLOGY   la ecologia

EXCITEMENT	la aventura
EXERCISE	el ejercicio
FEMINISM	el feminismo
FILM	el cine
GETTING HOME SAFELY	el llegar a salvo a casa.
HAPPINESS	la felicidad.
INCONSEQUENTIAL MATTERS, TO YOU, PROBABLY	
asuntos de poca importancia, para usted, probablemente	
LIBERAL CAUSES	causas liberales
LIFE, LIBERTY, AND THE PURSUIT OF HAPPINESS	
la vida, la libertad y la búsqueda de la felicidad	
MONEY	el dinero
MUSIC	la música
NOTHING MUCH	nada de particular
POETRY	la poesía
POLITICS	la política
POWER	el poder
QUIET	la tranquilidad
READING	la lectura
RELIGION	la religión
SAVING THE WORLD	un modo de salvar al mundo
SEX	el sexo
SPORTS	los deportes
THE PERFECT WAVE	la ola perfecta
THE THEATER	el teatro
THEATRICS	el drama
TRUTH	la verdad
VAGARIES OF THE UNIVERSE	los caprichos del universo
YOU	usted. *formal*
	tú. *familiar*

FASCINATING!

    ¡Fascinante!

I DO NOT BELIEVE IT.

    No lo creo.

WHAT ASTROLOGICAL SIGN ARE YOU?

    ¿Cuál es su signo del zodíaco?

        WHAT IS YOUR RISING SIGN?

          ¿Cuál es su signo ascendente?

AQUARIUS	Acuario
PISCES	Piscis
ARIES	Aries
TAURUS	Tauro
GEMINI	Geminis
CANCER	Cáncer
LEO	Leo
VIRGO	Virgo
LIBRA	Libra
SCORPIO	Escorpión
SAGITARRIUS	Sagitario
CAPRICORN	Capricornio

I DON'T KNOW WHAT YOU'RE TALKING ABOUT.

    No sé de que está hablando usted.

WHAT KIND OF WOMAN DO YOU ENJOY?

    ¿Qué clase de mujer le gusta a usted?

I AM MORE INTERESTED IN INTELLIGENCE

                    Me intereso más por <u>la inteligencia</u>

      CHARM   el encanto

      HUMOR   el humor

      SEX   el sexo

THAN I AM IN CHARM ...   que por el encanto...

      INTELLIGENCE   la inteligencia

      HUMOR   el humor

      SEX.   el sexo.

ARE YOU TRYING TO GET OVER A ROMANCE?

      ¿Trata usted de olvidar una relación amorosa?

I AM TRYING TO GET OVER A ROMANCE.

      Estoy tratando de olvidar una intriga amorosa.

HOW ROMANTIC.

      ¡Qué romántico!

I AM NOT ROMANTIC.

      No soy romántica.

ARE YOU MARRIED?

      ¿Está usted casado?

I AM MARRIED.

      Soy casada.

I AM NOT MARRIED.

      No soy casada.

SORT OF.

      Más o menos.

FORTUNATELY, NO.

    Afortunadamente, no.

UNFORTUNATELY, NO.

    Desgraciadamente, no.

I AM SINGLE

    Soy soltera

            BUT LIVING WITH SOMEONE.

              pero vivo con alguien.

I AM SEPARATED.

            Estoy _separada._

    DIVORCED   divorciada

    WIDOWED   soy viuda.

DO YOU HAVE ANY CHILDREN?

    ¿Tiene usted hijos?

FORTUNATELY, NO.

    Afortunadamente, no.

UNFORTUNATELY, NO.

    Desgraciadamente, no.

I HAVE ONE CHILD.

            Tengo una hija _fem_   un hijo _masc._

    TWO   dos hijos

    THREE   tres hijos

    MANY CHILDREN.   muchos hijos.

ARE YOU HOMOSEXUAL?

    ¿Es usted homosexual?

I AM HOMOSEXUAL.

Soy homosexual.

I AM NOT HOMOSEXUAL.

No soy homosexual.

I MIGHT BECOME HOMOSEXUAL SOON.

Es posible que yo llegue a ser pronto homosexual.

IT IS NONE OF YOUR BUSINESS.

No se ocupe usted de lo que no le incumbe.

GUESS.

Adivine usted.

DO YOU CONSIDER YOURSELF A FEMINIST?

¿Se considera usted feminista?

SEXIST?   sexista?

WOULD YOU LIKE TO DISCUSS IT?

¿Le gustaría discutirlo?

IS THERE A FEMINIST ORGANIZATION HERE?

¿Hay una organización feminista por aquí?

IS IT POSSIBLE TO MEET SOME FEMINIST WOMEN?

¿Es posible conocer a unas feministas?

FEMINIST MEN?   unos feministas?

DO YOU THINK THAT MEN AND WOMEN SHOULD BE EDUCATED THE
SAME?

¿Cree usted que los hombres y las mujeres deben tener la
misma educación?

PAID THE SAME   recibir el mismo sueldo?

TREATED THE SAME   recibir el mismo
tratamiento?

WHY NOT?
>   ¿Por qué no?

OF COURSE!
>   ¡Por supuesto!

THAT IS CONTRARY TO THE LAWS OF NATURE.
>   Eso va contra las leyes de la naturaleza.

YOU LOOK BEAUTIFUL WHEN YOU'RE ANGRY.
>   Usted se ve <u>muy guapo cuando está enojado</u>.   *to a man*
>   muy bonita cuando está enojada.   *to a woman*

IT SEEMS WE HAVE LITTLE IN COMMON.
>   Parece que tenemos muy poco en común.

IT SEEMS WE HAVE MUCH IN COMMON.
>   Parece que tenemos mucho en común.

IN YOUR COUNTRY, ARE MOST MEN LIKE YOU?
>   ¿En su patria son la mayor parte de los hombres como usted?

IN MY COUNTRY, MOST WOMEN ARE LIKE ME.
>   En mi patria la mayor parte de las mujeres son como yo.

SHALL WE SEE EACH OTHER AGAIN?
>   ¿Nos veremos otra vez?

WHAT A RIDICULOUS IDEA!
>   ¡Qué idea tan <u>ridícula!</u>

HOPELESS!	desesperada!
HORRIBLE!	horrible!
INSPIRED!	genial!

WHERE SHALL WE MEET?

   ¿Dónde nos encontraremos?

AT MY PLACE.

   Donde vivo yo.

AT YOUR PLACE.

   Donde vive usted.

IN PUBLIC.

   En un sitio público.

HOW ABOUT A LARGE CAFE?

      ¿Por qué no nos encontramos en un café grande?

SOMEWHERE WHERE WE CAN BE ALONE

     algún lugar donde podamos estar solos

A DIVE   un cabaret de mala fama

SOMEWHERE REDOLENT OF UNRESTRAINED PASSION & INTRIGUE

   algún lugar lleno de pasion desenfrenada y de intriga

A PLACE WITH LIVE MUSIC

      algún lugar donde haya música en vivo

A RESTAURANT FAVORED BY WEAK-STOMACHED TOURISTS

  un restaurante preferido por los turistas de digestión delicada

A PLACE WHERE YOU'D TAKE YOUR PARENTS

  un restaurante a donde llevaría usted a sus padres

ANYWHERE WITH A VIEW

  algún lugar donde haya una bella vista

HOW ABOUT SURPRISING ME   sorpréndame usted!

I BEG YOUR PARDON.

    Perdóneme usted.

WHEN SHALL WE MEET?

    ¿Cuándo nos encontraremos?

THE EARLIER THE BETTER.

    Lo más pronto posible.

THE LATER THE BETTER.

    Lo más tarde posible.

SHALL I BRING A CHAPERONE?

    ¿Debo llevar a un acompañante?

YOU ARE TOO FUNNY.

    ¡Qué <u>gracioso</u> es usted. *masc.*

        graciosa *fem.*

I'VE ALWAYS DEPENDED UPON THE KINDNESS OF STRANGERS.

    Siempre he dependido de la amabilidad de extraños.

IS THAT FROM A PLAY?

    ¿Es esa frase de una pieza de teatro?

THAT IS FROM A PLAY.

    Es de una pieza de teatro.

YOU ARE TOO CLEVER.

    Usted es muy <u>mañoso</u>. *masc.*

        mañosa. *f em.*

GOODBYE FOR NOW.

    Hasta luego.

SLEEPING ARRANGEMENTS

IS THERE A CHEAP HOTEL NEARBY?

                    ¿Hay un hotel <u>barato</u> por aquí?

CLEAN   limpio

IS THERE A GOOD HOTEL NEARBY?

       ¿Hay un buen hotel por aquí?

WHERE IS THE NEAREST YOUTH HOSTEL?

       ¿Hay un albergue para jóvenes cerca de aquí?

DO YOU KNOW WHERE I COULD RENT A ROOM?

       ¿Sabe usted dónde <u>puedo</u> alquilar una habitación?

WE   podemos

FOR HOW MANY DAYS?

       ¿Por cuántos días?

JUST FOR TONIGHT.

       Sólo para esta noche.

FOR A WEEK.   FOR A MONTH.

       Por una semana.   Por un mes.

HOW MUCH DOES THE ROOM COST PER NIGHT?

       ¿Quál es el precio de la habitación por noche?

IS IT QUIET?

       ¿Es una habitación tranquila?

DOES IT HAVE A NICE VIEW?

       ¿Hay una buena vista?

I'D LIKE SOMETHING THAT EVOKES THE ROMANCE OF AGES PAST.

Me gustaría algo que evoque el encanto de épocas pasadas.

I HAVE JUST THE ROOM FOR YOU.

Tengo la habitación perfecta para usted.

I'M SORRY; WE HAVE MODERNIZED.

Siento mucho; hemos modernizado el hotel.

I WANT A PRIVATE BATH.

Yo quisiera un cuarto de baño privado.

I DO NOT WANT A PRIVATE BATH.

No necesito un cuarto de baño privado.

WE WOULD LIKE A DOUBLE BED.

Quisiéramos una cama matrimonial.

WE WOULD LIKE TWIN BEDS.

Quisiéramos camas gemelas.

IS BREAKFAST INCLUDED?

¿Está incluido el desayuno?

MAY I SEE THE ROOM, PLEASE?

¿Puedo ver la habitación, por favor?

HAVE YOU ANY OTHERS?

¿Hay otras habitaciones?

THANK YOU FOR YOUR TROUBLE.

Muchas gracias por su atención.

FINE, I'LL TAKE IT.

    Muy bien, <u>voy a tomarla.</u>

WE'LL TAKE IT.   vamos a tomarla.

WHEN IS CHECK OUT TIME?

    ¿A qué hora hay que desocuparla?

I WOULD LIKE SOME SOAP, PLEASE.

    Quisiera tener <u>jabón</u>, por favor.

TOWELS	toallas, por favor
SOME DRINKING WATER	una botella de agua
A BLANKET	una manta
SOME QUIET	necesito tranquilidad y silencio.

THE KEY TO ROOM _____, PLEASE.

    La llave de mi habitación, por favor.

ARE THERE ANY MESSAGES FOR ME?

    ¿Hay algún recado para mí?

I AM EXPECTING A VISITOR.

    Espero unas visitas.

COME IN.

    Pase usted.

INTIMACIES

HOW GOOD TO SEE YOU.
>¡Qué gusto de verte!

MY DEAR.
>Querido mío *masc.*
>>Querida mía *fem.*

HOW ARE YOU?
>¿Cómo estás?

I AM WONDERFUL

	Estoy <u>muy bien.</u>
TERRIBLE	horrible
AS YOU SEE	como me ves
NERVOUS	nerviosa
EAGER	anhelosa
TIRED	cansada

TIRED BUT NOT TOO TIRED
>cansada pero no demasiado cansada

BUT PUTTY IN YOUR HANDS
>no soy más que masilla en tus manos

A SHADOW OF MY FORMER SELF.
>una sombra de mi ser anterior.

LET ME BE THE JUDGE OF THAT.
>Déjame a mi juzgar eso.

YOU FOOL.
>¡Tonto!*masc*
>>¡Tonta¡*fem*

117

DO YOU MIND IF I LOCK THE DOOR?

¿Me permites <u>cerrar con llave la puerta?</u>

PULL THE CURTAINS CLOSED	correr las cortinas
PULL THE CURTAINS OPEN	abrir las cortinas
SEND THE SERVANTS AWAY	despedir a los criados
MAKE MYSELF COMFORTABLE	acomodarme
DOUSE THE INCENSE?	apagar el incienso
TURN DOWN THE VOLUME	bajar el volumen sonoro
TURN UP THE VOLUME	aumentar el volumen sonoro
RECONSIDER	reconsiderar

INTRODUCE YOU TO A FRIEND.

presentarte a una amiga mía *fem.*

un amigo mío *masc.*

SHALL WE UNDRESS?

¿Nos desnudamos ahora?

SHALL WE NOT UNDRESS?

¿No nos desnudamos ahora?

LET'S NOT HURRY.

No tengamos prisa.

LET'S NOT WASTE TIME.

No perdamos tiempo.

ARE YOU CLEAN?

Espero que no tengas ninguna enfermedad.

DO YOU KNOW WHAT I MEAN?

¿Sabes lo que quiero decir?

ARE YOU SURE?

¿Estás seguro? *masc.*   segura *fem.*

I CONSIDER THAT AN INSULT.

    Considero eso un insulto.

I'M SURE YOU DO.

    Sin duda.

I LOVE YOUR EYES.

                 Me encantan <u>tus ojos.</u>

HAIR	tu pelo
MOUTH	tu boca
TONGUE	tu lengua
FACE	tu cara
RIGHT SHOULDER	tu hombro derecho
SKIN	tu cutis
STOMACH	tu vientre
SMELL	tu olor
UNDERWEAR	tu ropa interior
ENERGY	tu energía
PERSISTENCE	tu persistencia
FEET	tus pies
IMPERFECTIONS	tus imperfecciones

I LOVE YOU.

    Te amo.

I LOVE YOU, BUT I DON'T LIKE YOU.

    Te amo, pero no te encuentro simpático .

I LIKE YOU, BUT I DON'T LOVE YOU.

    Te encuentro simpatico, pero no te amo.

YOUR KISSES ARE DIVINE.

          Tus besos son <u>divinos</u>

    UNUSUAL   originales.

THIS IS MY FIRST TIME.

Es la primera vez para mí.

IS THIS YOUR FIRST TIME?

¿Es ésta la primera vez para ti?

I CONSIDER THAT AN INSULT.

Considero eso un insulto.

I FIND THAT DIFFICULT TO BELIEVE.

Me es difícil creerlo.

HAVE YOU CHANGED YOUR MIND?

¿Has cambiado de opinión?

NOT EXACTLY.

No completamente.

I HAVE CHANGED MY MIND.

He cambiado de opinión.

PERHAPS WE CAN BE FRIENDS.

Tal vez podamos ser amigos.

I MUST MAKE CERTAIN I WILL NOT GET PREGNANT.

Debo asegurarme de no quedar encinta.

I DIDN'T MEAN THAT.

Eso no es lo que yo quería decir.

AM I HURTING YOU?

¿Te estoy lastimando?

YES.

    Sí.

NO.

    No.

A LITTLE.

    Un poco.

SURELY YOU JEST.

    Tú bromeas, verdad?

WE ARE LIKE TWO SHIPS PASSING IN THE NIGHT.

    Somos como <u>dos barcos que se cruzan por la noche.</u>

A PAIR OF LOVE BIRDS	dos tórtolos inseparables
A SYMPHONY OF THE SENSES	una sinfonía de los sentidos
A BAD MOVIE	una mala película.

HOW ORIGINAL!

    ¡Qué original!

WHY ARE YOU READING FROM THE LITTLE BOOK?

    ¿Por qué consultas ese librito?

DO YOU LIKE THIS?

    ¿Te gusta esto?

WHAT?

    ¿Qué?

I DO NOT LIKE THAT.

    No me gusta eso.

I LIKE THAT.

    Me gusta eso.

ONE MORE TIME.

Una vez más.

LET ME DO THAT.

Déjame hacer eso.

WHAT ABOUT ME?

¿Y yo, pues?

I FORGOT.

Se me olvidó.

PATIENCE IS A VIRTUE.

La paciencia es una virtud.

HOW EXQUISITE!

¡Qué exquisito!

IT DOESN'T MATTER.

No importa.

MY DEAR.

querido mío *masc.*

querida mía *fem.*

THAT TICKLES.

¡Siento cosquillas!

I'M NOT LAUGHING AT YOU.

No me río de ti.

THERE IS NO BETTER PLACE TO LAUGH THAN IN BED.

No hay mejor lugar para la risa que la cama.

WHAT IS SO FUNNY?

¿Qué es tan cómico?

EVERYTHING / NOTHING.

 Todo /   nada.

THAT WAS MY FIRST TIME.

 Esa fue la primera vez para mí.

WAS THAT YOUR FIRST TIME?

 ¿Y esa fue la primera vez para tí?

I FIND THAT DIFFICULT TO BELIEVE.

 Me es difícil creerlo.

LET'S GO TO SLEEP.

 ¡Vamos a dormirnos!

     LET'S NOT GO TO SLEEP.

      No nos durmamos.

IT'S A PITY WE DON'T SPEAK THE SAME LANGUAGE.

 Es una lástima que no hablemos la misma lengua.

I'M GLAD WE SPEAK THE SAME LANGUAGE.

 Me alegro de que hablemos la misma lengua.

ARE YOU TIRED?

 ¿Estás cansado? *spoken to a man*

    estás cansada *spoken to a woman.*

I AM TIRED.

 Estoy cansada .

I NEVER TIRE.

 No me canso nunca.

GOOD MORNING!   ¡Buenos días!